ChemLab

TESTS

Atlantic Europe Publishing

First published in 1998 by Atlantic Europe Publishing Company Limited, Greys Court Farm, Greys Court, Henley-on-Thames, Oxon, RG9 4PG, UK.

Author
Brian Knapp, BSc, PhD
Project consultant
*Keith B. Walshaw, MA, BSc, DPhil
(Head of Chemistry, Leighton Park School)*
Project Director
Duncan McCrae, BSc
Editor
Mary Sanders, BSc
Special photography
Ian Gledhill
Electronic page make-up
The Ascenders Partnership
Designed and produced by
EARTHSCAPE EDITIONS
Print consultants
Chromo Litho Ltd
Reproduced in Malaysia by
Global Colour
Printed and bound in Italy by
L.E.G.O. SpA

Suggested cataloguing location
Knapp, Brian
  Tests
  ISBN 1 869860 77 2
  – ChemLab series, volume 12
540

Picture credits
All photographs are from the **Earthscape Editions** photolibrary except the following:
(c=centre t=top b=bottom l=left r=right)
Mary Evans Picture Library 6tr, 7br

This product is manufactured from sustainable managed forests. For every tree cut down at least one more is planted.

Contents

HOW TO USE THIS BOOK

These two pages show you how to get the most from this book.

❶ THE CONTENTS

Use the table of contents to see how this book is divided into themes. Each theme may have one or more demonstrations.

❷ THEMES

Each theme begins with a theory section on yellow-coloured paper. Major themes may contain several pages of theory for the demonstrations that are presented on the subsequent pages. They also contain biographies of scientists, whose work was important in the understanding of the theme.

❸ DEMONSTRATIONS

Demonstrations are at the heart of any chemistry study. However, many demonstrations cannot easily be shown to a whole class for health and safety reasons, because the demonstration requires a close-up view, because it is over too quickly, takes too long to complete, or because it requires special apparatus. The demonstrations shown here have been photographed especially to overcome these problems and give you a very close-up view of the key stages in each reaction.

The text, pictures and diagrams are closely connected. To get the best from the demonstration, look closely at each picture as soon as its reference occurs in the text.

Many of the pictures show enlarged views of parts of the demonstration to help you see exactly what is happening. Notice, too, that most pictures form part of a sequence. You will find that it pays to look at the picture sequence more than once, and always be careful to make sure you can see exactly what is described in any picture before you move on.

The main heading for a demonstration or a set of demonstrations.

An introduction expands on the heading, summarising the demonstration or group of demonstrations and their context in the theme.

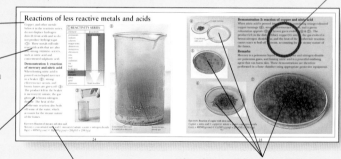

Each demonstration is carefully explained and illustrated with photographs and, where necessary, with diagrams, tables and graphs. The illustrations referred to are numbered ①, ②, ③, etc.

Chemical equations are shown where appropriate (see the explanation of equations at the bottom of page 5).

The photographs show the key stages that you might see if you witness a demonstration at first-hand. Examine them very carefully against the text description.

APPARATUS

The demonstrations have been carefully conducted as representative examples of the main chemical processes. The apparatus used is standard, but other choices are possible and you may see different equipment in your laboratory, so make sure you understand the principles behind the apparatus selected. The key pieces of apparatus are defined in the glossary.

❹ GLOSSARY OF TECHNICAL TERMS

Words with which you may be unfamiliar are shown in small capitals where they first occur in the text. Use the glossary on pages 66–74 to find more information about these technical words. Over 400 items are presented alphabetically.

oxidising agent: a substance that removes electrons from another substance being oxidised (and therefore is itself reduced) in a redox reaction. *Example:* chlorine (Cl_2).

❺ INDEX TO ALL VOLUMES IN THE SET

To look for key words in any of the 12 volumes that make up the ChemLab set, use the Master Index on pages 75 to 80. The instructions on page 75 show you how to cross-reference between volumes.

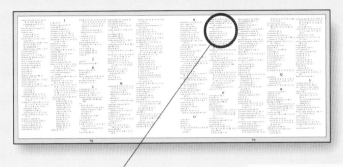

The most important locations of the term 'oxidising agent' are given in a master index which includes references to all of the volumes in the ChemLab set.

ABBREVIATIONS

Units are in the international metric system. Some units of measurement are abbreviated, or shortened, as follows:
°C = degrees Celsius
km = kilometre
m = metre
cm = centimetre
mm = millimetre
sq m = square metre
g = gram
kg = kilogram
kJ = kilojoule
l = litre

❻ CHEMICAL EQUATIONS

Important or relevant chemical equations are shown in written and symbolic form together with additional information.

What the reaction equation illustrates

Word equation

Symbol equation
The symbols for each element can be found in any Periodic Table.

Where relevant, the oxidation state is shown as Roman numerals in brackets.

EQUATION: Reaction of copper and nitric acid

Copper + nitric acid ⇨ copper(II) nitrate + water + nitrogen dioxide

$Cu(s) + 4HNO_3(conc) ⇨ Cu(NO_3)_2(aq) + 2H_2O(l) + 2NO_2(g)$
Blue

The two halves of the chemical equation are separated by the arrow that shows the progression of the reaction. Each side of the equation must balance.

Sometimes additional descriptions are given below the symbol equation.

The symbol indicating the state of each substance is shown as follows:
(s) = solid
(g) = gaseous
(l) = liquid
(aq) = aqueous
(conc) = concentrated

The correct number of atoms, ions and molecules and their proportions in any compound are shown by the numbers. A free electron is shown as an e^-.

TESTS FOR ACIDITY

ACIDS and BASES are related chemical COMPOUNDS. They have been known since ancient times. Acids were known to have a sour taste and to CORRODE some metals. Bases (ALKALIS if they dissolve in water) were known to have a bitter taste and to be slippery and soapy to the touch. It was also discovered that acids and bases affect the colour of some natural organic substances, such as the juice extracted from crushed cabbage and from litmus. However, until the 19th century, nobody had a clear theory about what acids and bases are or how to test for them accurately.

In the early part of the 19th century, Sir Humphry Davy in Britain and Joseph L. Gay-Lussac and Louis J. Thénard in France demonstrated that the acidity of a compound is related to the presence of hydrogen. This allowed the German chemist, Justus von Liebig, to define an acid as a compound that contains hydrogen in a form that can be replaced by a metal.

With this information, by the later part of the 19th century, the Swedish chemist, Svante Arrhenius, was able to conclude that acids and bases in water (in AQUEOUS SOLUTION) form electrically charged particles known as IONS. This meant that an acid is a substance that ionises in water to yield hydrogen ions (H^+), and that a substance which ionises in water to produce hydroxide ions (OH^-) is a base (alkali) $H^+(aq) + OH^-(aq)$ $H_2O(l)$. An acid can donate hydrogen ions whereas a base can accept them. (Testing for ions is described on page 46 onwards.)

(Testing for ions is described on page 46 onwards.)

GREAT EXPERIMENTAL SCIENTISTS
Sir Humphry Davy

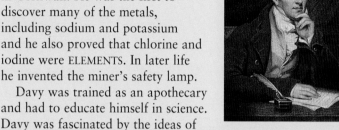

Sir Humphry Davy (1778–1829) was a famous English chemist born in Cornwall. He was the first to discover many of the metals, including sodium and potassium and he also proved that chlorine and iodine were ELEMENTS. In later life he invented the miner's safety lamp.

Davy was trained as an apothecary and had to educate himself in science. Davy was fascinated by the ideas of another famous scientist, Antoine L. Lavoisier, and he began to experiment with light and heat. In 1801 he was asked to become the chemistry lecturer at the newly established Royal Institution of Great Britain in London. Over the following years, Davy made some remarkable discoveries and also was a very popular lecturer. One of those who went to his lectures was Michael Faraday, who was later made Davy's assistant before going on to be one of the greatest experimental scientists of all time.

Just a year before Davy was made lecturer in chemistry, Alessandro Volta made the world's first BATTERY. Davy used a battery to dissociate water into oxygen and hydrogen, in a process called ELECTROLYSIS. It was his experimentation with electricity that determined the path of Davy's investigations. In 1808, Davy isolated the METALS, sodium and potassium, electrically. In 1810 he experimented with acids and reasoned that hydrogen was a common element in all acids.

He also produced nitrous oxide (dinitrogen oxide, 'laughing gas'), by heating ammonium nitrate. Years later it was to be used as a dental anaesthetic. He designed the arc lamp for intense white lighting, he produced a method for DESALINATING sea water and he invented CATHODIC PROTECTION for ships' hulls.

Davy was knighted for his scientific work and also became president of the Royal Society of Great Britain in London.

Acid–base strengths

It was this new understanding that allowed chemists to suggest that acids and bases could have different strengths and that these strengths were related to the concentration of hydrogen ions. From this came the idea of pH, an acid–base scale which covers the whole range of solutions of acids and alkalis.

The discovery that acids and alkalis are ELECTROLYTES, and that their solutions conduct electricity, was a vital step in allowing scientists to find a way to measure pH accurately. The pH meter measures the concentration of hydrogen ions in solution. The meter reading from a probe dipped into an electrolyte gives a very accurate reading of pH.

The pH scale

pH is measured on a logarithmic scale, and it shows the concentration of hydrogen ions in the solution. At 25°C an acidic solution has a pH value of less than 7; an alkaline solution has a pH greater than 7; and a neutral solution has a pH equal to 7.

Indicators

It was discovered that some chemical substances change colour when they react with an acid or with an alkali. (The colour change is due to the addition or removal of a hydrogen ion.) These substances are called INDICATORS. One of the oldest indicators is litmus, a vegetable dye which is red in acids and blue in alkaline solutions. Another indicator is *p*-nitrophenol, which is colourless in acids and yellow in alkaline solutions.

However, each indicator tends to work best over a relatively narrow range of pH values. Some indicators – of which litmus is one – change between colours that are not very easy to distinguish. These problems have led to the gradual abandonment of litmus in favour of the combination of a number of brightly coloured indicators known as a Universal Indicator. This mixture of methyl orange, methyl red, bromothymol blue, and phenolphthalein, is dark green in neutral solution, and changes continuously from red to violet between pH 3 and pH 10 (see page 10).

GREAT EXPERIMENTAL SCIENTISTS
Svante Arrhenius

Svante Arrhenius (1859–1927) was a Swedish chemist who was interested in the effects of electricity in water. In 1884, he applied for a doctorate with a thesis that included the way in which an electrical current breaks up compounds. It was so revolutionary that the examiners at his university gave him the lowest grade for it! When, later, it was discovered to be correct, he was awarded a Nobel prize.

Arrhenius was able to build on the research into acids and bases to develop a new theory of how acids work and the role of hydrogen ions.

In 1889 Arrhenius also discovered that the rate of a chemical reaction often doubles with a 10°C rise in temperature.

Indicators made from vegetable extracts

Vegetable extracts are complex mixtures of many substances. Four hundred years ago, Sir Robert Boyle discovered that, by crushing a particular white lichen and treating the juice with alcohol, ammonia, lime, and potassium carbonate in the presence of air, he could get a solution that turned red in an acid, and purple in an alkaline solution. He had created the forerunner of litmus. In a similar way, some other vegetables can be used as acid–base indicators. Red cabbage extract is a common one.

Demonstration: litmus

For hundreds of years, litmus was the most commonly used indicator dye for measuring the acidity of a substance and differentiating between acids and alkalis.

Litmus is most commonly used as strips of litmus paper (①) or as strips of filter paper soaked in litmus solution. Sometimes litmus is used as a solution. The colour of neutral litmus solution is somewhere in-between blue and red (②). If acidified, it turns red (③ to ④). In alkaline solutions, it turns purple–blue (⑤). Unfortunately, the human eye cannot differentiate easily between slight changes of colour that occur in the red–blue range. This is one reason why litmus paper is used less now than it was in the past. Universal Indicator (see page 10) is more versatile and so is used more commonly now.

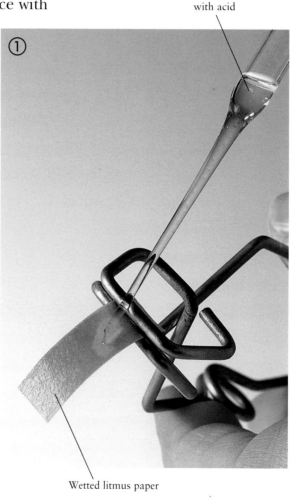

Pipette with acid

Wetted litmus paper

(Above) **Acid being dripped on to litmus paper**

Neutral

③

④

⑤

Partly acid

Acid

Alkaline

(Right and below) Red Cabbage extract is sometimes recommended as an indicator in home-based chemistry experiments. In this demonstration, red cabbage leaves were sliced and soaked in warm water to produce this simple indicator, which is deep purple when neutral. When hydrochloric acid is added, the indicator turns a bright red. When an alkali, in this case sodium hydroxide granules, is added, the indicator turns green.

Neutral

Acid

Alkaline

Universal Indicator

An important QUANTITATIVE way to measure acidity is to measure the pH, that is a measure of the concentration of the hydrogen ions in the solution.

An indicator will change colour at a specific pH, so a single indicator, such as litmus, cannot be used to measure the pH outside its range (around neutral). To get a range of colour changes, a number of indicator solutions are mixed together to give a Universal Indicator.

When neutral, Universal Indicator is deep green. In a strongly acidic solution it turns a deep red whilst, in a very alkaline solution, it turns purple-blue. A chart is used to show the gradation of colours that are produced by Universal Indicator and their corresponding pH values.

Because all chemical indicators rely on colour changes, they can only be used on colourless solutions. No coloured solutions can be tested in this way. Notice, too, that the accuracy of using colour indicators to show pH is quite limited. For example, the difference in colour of the indicator in a solution which is pH 7 as opposed to 8 is difficult to see. As a result, Universal Indicator is still used primarily for testing whether a colourless solution or gas is just acidic or alkaline. pH is also used in many field-testing kits, for example, for assessing the pH of agricultural soils. More accurate pH values can only be obtained by using a pH meter (see page 12).

The meaning of pH

The acidity of a solution depends on the relative number of hydrogen (H+) ions and hydroxide (OH−) ions in the solution. This number varies enormously between very acid and very alkaline solutions, so it is not possible to use a simple straight line (linear) scale to measure the concentration. Instead, the pH scale is a logarithmic scale, where each number on the scale represents a tenfold change in concentration. Thus a pH 5 solution has ten times the hydrogen ion concentration of a pH 6 solution, and a pH 4 solution has 100 times the concentration of hydrogen ions of a pH 6 solution. On this scale, a pH of 1 is very strongly acidic, a pH of 14 is very strongly alkaline, and a pH of 7 is neutral.

(Below) This chart shows the range of pH from a strong acid at pH 1 to a strong alkali at pH 14.

pH	1	2	3	4	5	6	7	8	9	10	11	12	13	14

Very strong acid   Weak acid   Neutral   Weak alkali   Very strong alkali

(Right) This chart shows the colour change for Universal Indicator in relation to pH.

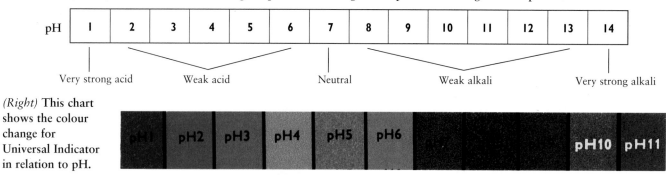

pH1   pH2   pH3   pH4   pH5   pH6   pH10   pH11

Litmus indicator	Phenolphthalein indicator	Methyl orange indicator	Bromothymol blue indicator

   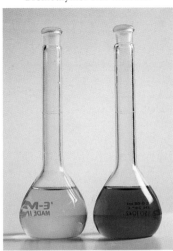

(Above) These flasks show the colour changes applicable to a number of indicators used in the laboratory. The left-hand flask of each pair shows the colour in an acidic solution whilst the right-hand flask shows the colour in an alkaline solution.

(Below) These are the colour changes shown by adding Universal Indicator solution to beakers containing colourless solutions of various acidities. Compare these with the colour chart on page 10 and with the pH meter tests on page 12 to see how accurate a measurement the colour change is.

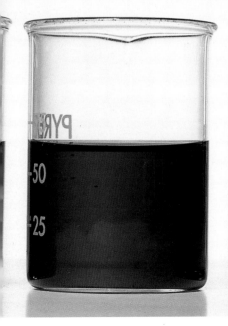 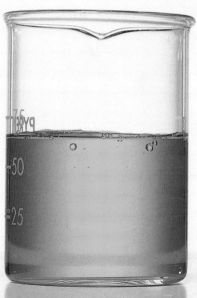  

11

Using a pH meter

Universal Indicator is used for an approximate determination of the pH of a colourless solution. However, instead of using chemicals, which change colour, to find an approximate pH of a solution, it is possible to use a pH meter to obtain a much more accurate determination of pH. In any case, if the solution you are trying to measure is coloured, a Universal Indicator cannot be used.

Demonstration: setting up the pH meter

The pH meter consists of a meter and a probe. The probe is placed in the solution to be tested. Since cross-contamination will occur if the probe is taken directly from one solution into another, it is vital that the probe is thoroughly washed in distilled water in-between tests.

The pH meter has to be calibrated before use. This involves using two BUFFER solutions. These are solutions that are resistant to changing pH. The buffers are made up using tablets, which are dropped into water and allowed to dissolve. Buffer solutions

(Below) pH meter being used to find the exact pH of solutions whose approximate acidity and alkalinity are given by the Universal Indicator solutions.

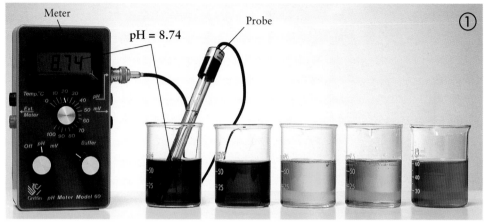

Meter   Probe
pH = 8.74   ①

pH = 8.02   ②

pH = 8.74   pH = 8.02   pH = 7.08   pH = 4.99   pH = 3.90   ③

pH = 8.39

④

pH = 8.74

pH = 8.02

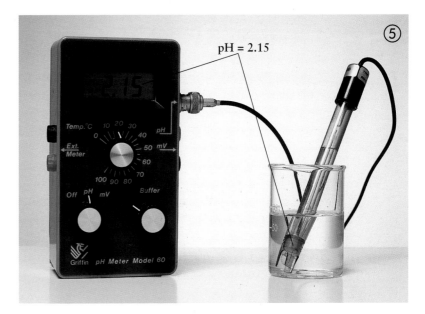

pH = 2.15

⑤

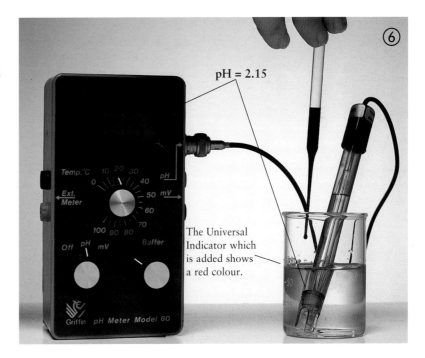

pH = 2.15

⑥

The Universal Indicator which is added shows a red colour.

are made up to have known pH values from near the ends of the pH range.

In this demonstration, the pH values of a number of aqueous solutions are being measured (① & ②). The solutions have been prepared and 2% Universal Indicator has been added so that you can see the approximate pH to be expected. To make sure that accurate comparisons are being made, the concentration of the indicator in the solutions is kept the same. The pH values of the solutions as determined by the meter are also shown (③).

Three beakers of approximately the same colour are shown to have different pH values (④). The left-hand one reads 8.73, the middle one 8.39 and the right-hand one 8.02.

An unknown colourless solution is tested and found to have a pH of 2.15 (⑤), showing it to be strongly acidic. This is then confirmed in an approximate way by dropping some (green) Universal Indicator into the solution and watching it turn red (⑥).

Tests for water and water vapour

Water is the most common chemical SOLVENT and many liquids are AQUEOUS solutions. Water may also be present in solids as WATER OF CRYSTALLISATION and as a VAPOUR in many gaseous mixtures.

The many cases in which water is present both make it likely that the presence of water will need to be tested, and also suggest that a range of tests will be needed.

Demonstration: test for water vapour

Some substances will absorb water vapour very readily. They can therefore be used as DRYING AGENTS in many practical experiments. If a gas containing water vapour is passed over granules of a drying agent, the drying agent will absorb water. It is possible to weigh the drying agent before and after the passage of water vapour, but it is often sufficient just to prove that water vapour is present. It is easiest to use a drying agent that also changes colour as it absorbs water, such as purplish-blue, ANHYDROUS cobalt chloride (①), which turns pink as it HYDRATES (②), or white, anhydrous copper sulphate (③), which turns blue as it hydrates (④). The most effective way to apply these tests is to cool the gas so that water vapour condenses on to the REACTANT.

In testing for water vapour, it is important to use very small amounts of testing agent because the smaller the amount, the faster it will absorb enough vapour to change colour.

Water added from a pipette

Anhydrous cobalt chloride

①

②

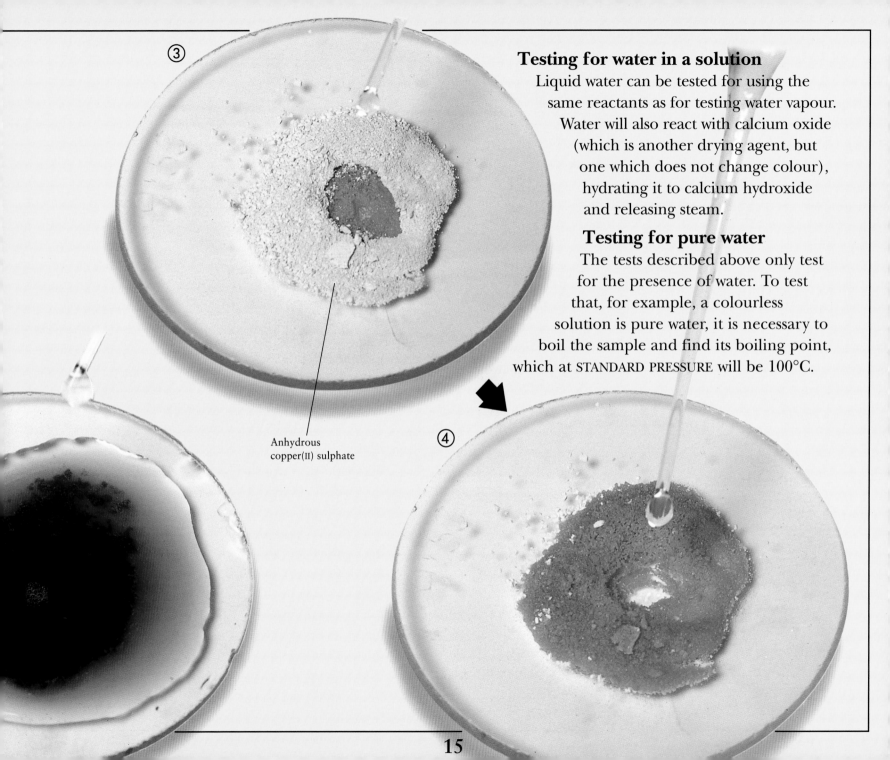

③

Testing for water in a solution

Liquid water can be tested for using the same reactants as for testing water vapour. Water will also react with calcium oxide (which is another drying agent, but one which does not change colour), hydrating it to calcium hydroxide and releasing steam.

Testing for pure water

The tests described above only test for the presence of water. To test that, for example, a colourless solution is pure water, it is necessary to boil the sample and find its boiling point, which at STANDARD PRESSURE will be 100°C.

Anhydrous
copper(II) sulphate

④

15

Tests for an oxidising agent

Many OXIDISING AGENTS can be found in the laboratory. For example, potassium permanganate and hydrogen peroxide are both powerful oxidising agents. Active non-metals, such as chlorine and oxygen, are all good oxidising agents because they form negative ions easily.

An oxidising agent causes another substance to be oxidised. A substance has been oxidised in a chemical reaction when oxygen has been added or hydrogen removed from it, but most specifically when it loses electrons. When OXIDATION takes place in a reaction, REDUCTION (the opposite process) must also occur and so an oxidising agent is itself reduced.

Because the processes of reduction and oxidation necessarily occur together in such reactions, they are called REDOX reactions.

Tests for a reducing agent can be seen on page 18.

Demonstration 1: test for an oxidising agent using acidified potassium iodide

To test for an oxidising agent, drop some of the substance under examination into colourless potassium iodide solution which is acidified with sulphuric acid (①).

If an oxidising agent is present, the result is first yellow, then brown, iodine which may precipitate (②). The oxidising agent has oxidised the colourless iodide to a brown iodine PRECIPITATE. In this demonstration, the oxidising agent under test was colourless hydrogen peroxide (H_2O_2), which is reduced to water.

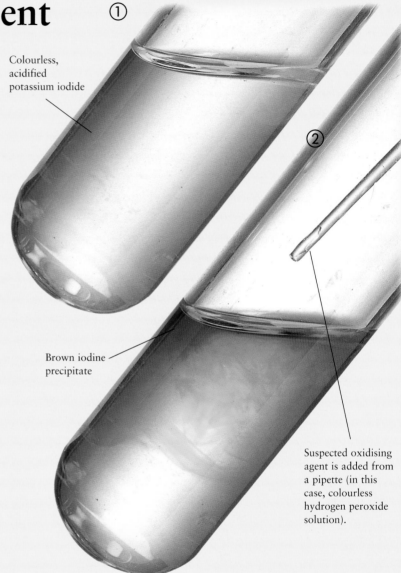

① Colourless, acidified potassium iodide

②

Brown iodine precipitate

Suspected oxidising agent is added from a pipette (in this case, colourless hydrogen peroxide solution).

EQUATION: Test for an oxidising agent

Hydrogen peroxide + potassium iodide + sulphuric acid ⇨ iodine + potassium sulphate + water

$H_2O_2(aq) + 2KI(aq) + H_2SO_4(aq) \Rightarrow I_2(s) + K_2SO_4(aq) + 2H_2O(l)$

Demonstration 2: test for an oxidising agent by adding starch

To make the test more sensitive to small quantities of an oxidising agent, another reagent, starch, is added to the acidified potassium iodide solution (③). The result is the formation of a dark blue precipitate (④). Because the blue colour is much more intense than the brown, it is easier to observe the change in the test tube.

The two results are shown here side by side (⑤).

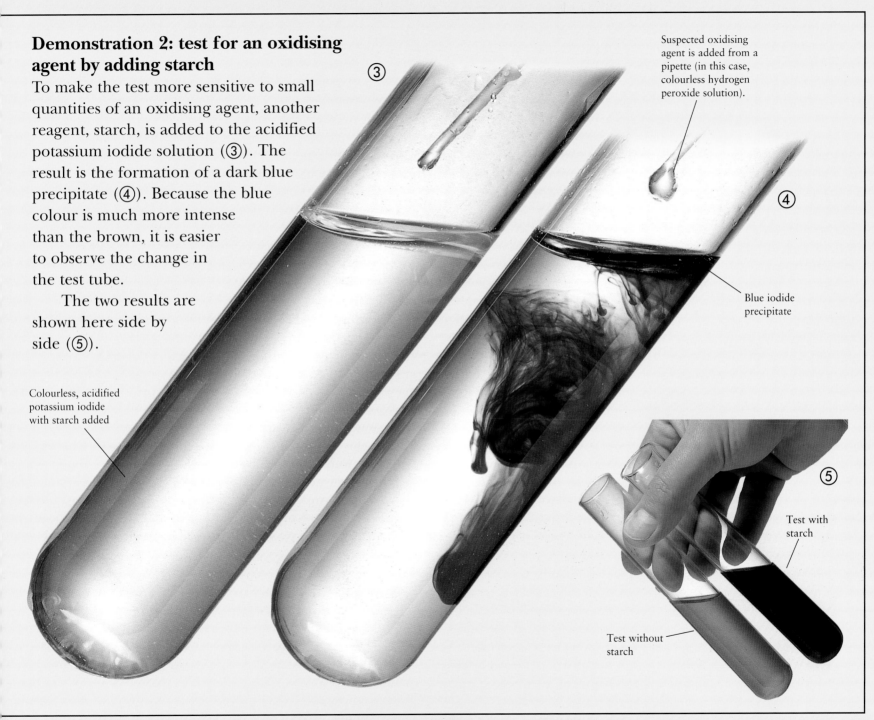

③

Suspected oxidising agent is added from a pipette (in this case, colourless hydrogen peroxide solution).

④

Blue iodide precipitate

Colourless, acidified potassium iodide with starch added

⑤

Test with starch

Test without starch

Tests for a reducing agent

A reducing agent causes another substance to be reduced. A substance has been reduced in a chemical reaction when oxygen has been removed or hydrogen added to it, but most specifically when it gains electrons.

Many reducing agents can be found in the laboratory. For example, sulphur dioxide is a powerful reducing agent. The ALKALI METALS are strong reducing agents because they easily form positive ions.

When reduction takes place in a reaction, oxidation (the opposite process) must also occur and so a reducing agent is itself oxidised. Tests for an oxidising agent can be seen on page 16.

Demonstration 1: test for a reducing agent using acidified potassium permanganate

Potassium permanganate is a rich source of oxygen and so is easily reduced. A reducing agent will change the colour of acidified potassium permanganate from purple to black, green, pale pink or make it colourless.

A little sulphuric acid is added to a beaker of potassium permanganate solution (①) to act as a source of the hydrogen ions needed for the reaction.

Remarks

The amount of acid used is critical to the exact colour produced. With excess acid, and therefore with an excess supply of H^+ ions, the reaction proceeds from the purple permanganate (which is manganate(VII)), to colourless manganese(II); with insufficient acid, the

Suspected reducing agent (sodium sulphite)

Acidified potassium permanganate

reaction proceeds to black manganese(IV).

In an alkaline solution, and therefore with even fewer hydrogen ions, the reaction may proceed only to manganate(VI), which is green. Thus the colour of the solution at the end of the test will depend on the amount of acid added, but the reduction will always be marked by a colour change.

The reducing agent used in this demonstration was sodium sulphite (a white crystalline solid), which is readily oxidised to become sodium sulphate (also see preparation of sulphur dioxide gas on page 28). The sodium sulphite was dropped into the potassium permanganate solution (②). For test purposes, the

EQUATION: Reduction of potassium permanganate
Manganate(VII) ions + hydrogen ions from sulphuric acid + electrons from the reducing agent ⇨ manganese(II) + water
$$MnO_4^- + 8H^+ + 5e^- \Rightarrow Mn^{2+} + 4H_2O$$

contrast between the permanganate and its reduced form, manganese(II), is best shown by allowing the solution to remain unstirred so that the solution turns progressively more colourless from the bottom of the beaker (③, ④, ⑤ & ⑥).

Demonstration 2: test for a reducing gas using acidified potassium permanganate

A similar test using acidified potassium permanganate can be used for gases. For example, soaking a piece of filter paper in acidified potassium permanganate solution and holding it in a stream of hydrogen sulphide will turn the paper from purple to pale pink.

In the same way, bubbling the gas through a solution of acidified potassium manganate(VII) solution (⑦) will turn the solution from purple (⑧) to pale pink (⑨).

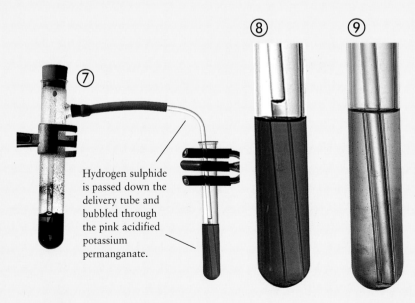

Hydrogen sulphide is passed down the delivery tube and bubbled through the pink acidified potassium permanganate.

TESTS FOR GASES

Gases are commonly produced by chemical reactions in the laboratory. Many gases are poisonous and preparations that involve poisonous gases and tests for them should be done in a fume chamber. For safety reasons, it is particularly necessary to understand the products of a chemical reaction by completing a balanced chemical equation before proceeding with the experiment.

Approaches to testing

In this section on testing gases, the reactions produce only small volumes of a gas, for testing purposes. One suitable piece of apparatus for testing is a side-arm boiling tube with a thistle funnel (①). The solid or liquid reactant is placed in the boiling tube and the liquid reactant poured on to it through the thistle funnel in modest quantities until the base of the funnel stem is covered and until sufficient gas is released for it to be tested.

Gases can be tested in a number of ways, one of the easiest of which is to observe its colour. The tests on the following pages are organised first by the colour of the gas (table opposite). The largest groups of gases are colourless (pages 22 to 36), then there are important brown gases (pages 37 to 40), violet gases (page 41) and greenish-yellow gases (pages 42 and 43).

SUMMARY OF PROPERTIES TO TEST FOR IN COMMON GASES

Because many gases are poisonous, testing the gas by smell is NOT recommended.

COLOURLESS GASES (pages 22 to 36)

Oxygen (O_2): Will relight a glowing splint. Unlike N_2O, it does not produce a brown gas on contact with air.

Hydrogen (H_2): Ignites in air on contact with a lighted splint to give a high pitched 'pop'.

Carbon dioxide (CO_2): Turns clear limewater cloudy. Excess carbon dioxide makes the solution turn clear again.

Carbon monoxide (CO): Burns in air with a blue flame and produces carbon dioxide that can be detected using limewater (as above).

Sulphur dioxide (SO_2): Acidic. Powerful reducing agent turning yellow potassium dichromate blue, acidified potassium permanganate pale pink, and colourless potassium iodide brown.

Hydrogen sulphide (H_2S): Acidic. Powerful reducing agent turning yellow potassium dichromate blue, acidified potassium permanganate pale pink, and colourless potassium iodide brown.

Hydrogen chloride (HCl): Strongly acidic. Reacts with ammonia gas (from concentrated ammonia solution) to produce a white smoke of ammonium chloride.

Ammonia (NH_3): The only common alkaline gas and so it turns damp pH paper blue. Reacts with hydrogen chloride gas to produce a white smoke of ammonium chloride.

Nitrogen monoxide (NO): Colourless but combines with oxygen in air to form brown fumes of nitrogen dioxide.

Hydrogen bromide (HBr): Colourless but frequently mixed with bromine gas, which is reddish-brown. Very strongly acidic and extremely corrosive in combination with bromine.

BROWN GASES (pages 37 to 40)

Bromine (Br_2): Acidic. A more powerful bleach than nitrogen dioxide. Colours water brown. Dissolves in methylbenzene to produce a reddish-brown solution.

Nitrogen dioxide (NO_2): Strongly acidic but a weaker bleach than bromine. Does not colour water in dilute solution.

VIOLET GASES (page 41)

Iodine (I_2): Dissolves in methylbenzene to produce a violet solution.

GREENISH-YELLOW GASES (pages 42 to 43)

Chlorine (Cl_2): Acidic but also a strong bleach. More powerful oxidising agent than iodine. Dissolves in methylbenzene to produce a greenish-yellow solution.

Within these broad categories, gases are tested for their acidity (②), their COMBUSTION with a glowing or lighted splint (③), how powerful they are as reducing or oxidising agents, and their density in comparison to, and reactivity, with air. Other specific tests may also be used.

Gases can be much more dangerous than liquids and solids. A gas will readily mix with air, spreading rapidly throughout a room. This is one reason why tests with poisonous gases must be done in the fume chamber. In some of these tests, you will see that the demonstrator is wearing protective gloves, indicating that the gas is harmful in some way, for example, CORROSIVE. Clamps are used where the protective gloves are not sufficient protection. Eye protection should always also be worn.

Any hazards associated with relevant gases are mentioned in the sections concerned.

③

(Left) A small amount of gas can be produced in a side-arm boiling tube. In this case, the gas is to be tested by bubbling it into a solution, so a delivery tube is used. The use of limewater as shown here is specific to testing for carbon dioxide, a safe gas not requiring the use of protective gloves.

①

②

(Above) The combustion of a gas can be tested using a glowing or lighted splint. In this case a glowing splint is relit, indicating that oxygen is most probably the gas being given off.

(Left) In general, a test for a gas needs a relatively small amount of gas and soaked filter paper is often more useful. This brown gas is being tested for acidity. The indicator must always be in solution. If the indicator is on a dry paper, the paper must first be wetted with distilled water.

Testing for oxygen (O₂)

Oxygen is a colourless gas that supports combustion.

Many oxygen-rich compounds will DECOMPOSE on heating to release oxygen. In this demonstration, the oxygen-rich compound being heated is potassium chlorate.

Demonstration: test for oxygen with a glowing splint

To test for the presence of oxygen, first light a wooden splint and then blow it out to leave a glowing ember at the tip. Introduce the glowing splint into the test tube containing the suspected oxygen (①). It is important not to let the splint touch the substance being heated at the bottom of the tube. If oxygen is present, the splint will immediately be rekindled and burst into flames (②).

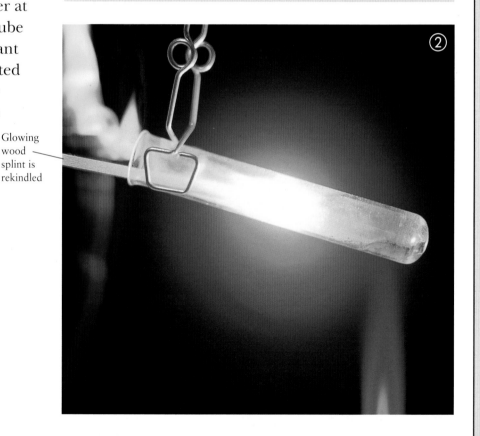

Glowing wood splint is rekindled

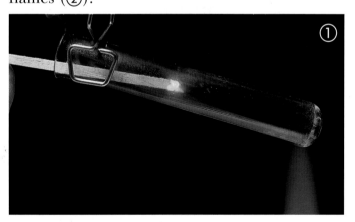

EQUATION: Decomposition of potassium chlorate

Potassium chlorate(I) ⇨ potassium chloride + oxygen

$2KClO_3(s) ⇨ 2KCl(s) + 3O_2(g)$

CATALYST, MnO_2

Testing for hydrogen (H$_2$)

Hydrogen is a colourless gas of low density that will ignite with a popping sound.

Demonstration: test for hydrogen using a lighted splint

Hydrogen does not support the combustion of a glowing splint so, if a glowing splint is plunged far into an inverted gas jar containing hydrogen, it is extinguished. However, hydrogen forms an explosive mixture in air, making the basis for a test.

When a long, lighted splint (①) is introduced into an inverted gas jar containing hydrogen, a small explosion occurs at the mouth of the jar where the hydrogen and air mix. This is heard as a loud, high-pitched 'popping' sound.

The splint goes out where it is entirely within the hydrogen (②), but the splint relights some way down its length at the point where the hydrogen and air are mixing and combusting (③).

In this demonstration, the hydrogen is generated by reacting hydrochloric acid with small pieces of zinc.

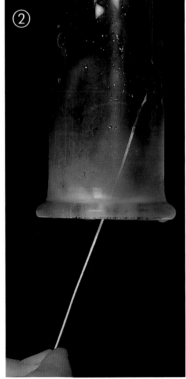

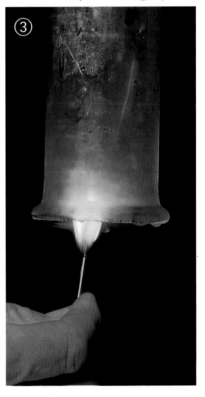

PROPERTIES OF HYDROGEN

Hydrogen is colourless and has no smell and is non-toxic.

Hydrogen is highly flammable, burning with a very hot, colourless flame, and may explode in air.

Hydrogen is the lightest chemical element known and has one-twelfth of the density of air.

There are more compounds of hydrogen than of any other element, because hydrogen combines with every element except the noble gases. Hydrogen comprises about 99.88% of the Universe, but because it is so light it escaped from the Earth's atmosphere long ago and now makes up only 0.75% of our planet in combination with other elements. On Earth, the vast majority of compounds formed with hydrogen are organic products derived from living organisms.

Hydrogen is not soluble in water at room temperature. Hydrogen is a reducing agent, reducing metal oxides to lower oxides or to the free metal.

In the laboratory, hydrogen is usually prepared by reacting an acid with a metal.

Testing for carbon dioxide (CO_2)

Carbon dioxide gas is colourless and weakly acidic. It is most easily identified using a solution of calcium hydroxide, a laboratory REAGENT usually known as limewater.

Demonstration: test for carbon dioxide

Carbon dioxide is bubbled through the limewater (①). The limewater turns cloudy as a result of the formation of small particles of the precipitate, calcium carbonate, which remain in suspension (②).

Remarks

A large amount of carbon dioxide bubbling rapidly through limewater may make the limewater turn cloudy and then clear again quite quickly (③). This is because the calcium carbonate precipitate is converted into soluble calcium hydrogen carbonate ($Ca(HCO_3)_2$) (calcium bicarbonate) by an excess of carbon dioxide. However, if this happens, then boiling the solution will turn it cloudy again, as the calcium hydrogen carbonate is converted back into calcium carbonate.

In this demonstration, carbon dioxide was produced by reacting hydrochloric acid with sodium carbonate.

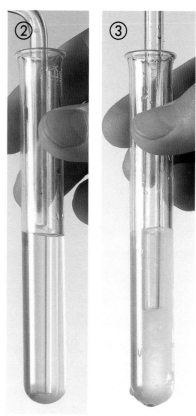

Limewater

PROPERTIES OF CARBON DIOXIDE

Carbon dioxide is a colourless gas with no smell and is not particularly reactive.

Carbon dioxide is commonly formed in the laboratory by the combustion in air of any material containing carbon but it is also formed in nature by the action of an acid on a carbonate, for example, rainwater on limestone. Since it is a product of complete combustion, carbon dioxide does not burn or support combustion.

Carbon dioxide is denser than air. Carbon dioxide is slightly soluble in water at room temperature forming a weak acid, carbonic acid (H_2CO_3).

Carbon dioxide makes up about 0.03% air in the Earth's atmosphere and is used by plants in photosynthesis.

EQUATION 1: Carbon dioxide generation by reacting an acid and a carbonate

Sodium carbonate + hydrochloric acid ⇨ sodium chloride + water + carbon dioxide

$$Na_2CO_3(s) + 2HCl(aq) \Rightarrow 2NaCl(aq) + H_2O(l) + CO_2(g)$$

EQUATION 2: Some carbon dioxide and limewater

Carbon dioxide + calcium hydroxide ⇨ calcium carbonate + water

$$CO_2(g) + Ca(OH)_2(aq) \Rightarrow CaCO_3(s) + H_2O(l)$$

EQUATION 3: Excess carbon dioxide and limewater

Calcium hydroxide + carbon dioxide + water ⇨ calcium hydrogen carbonate

$$CaCO_3(s) + CO_2(g) + H_2O(l) \Rightarrow Ca(HCO_3)_2(aq)$$

Carbon dioxide in breath

As shown on this page, limewater can be used to test for the presence of carbon dioxide in breath.

Blowing a stream of bubbles into limewater using a straw (④) produces a precipitate of fine particles of calcium carbonate which makes the solution cloudy and look almost like milk.

If you keep blowing through the straw, the solution quickly goes clear again (⑤) because the additional amount of carbon dioxide reacts with the calcium carbonate to produce soluble, and colourless, calcium hydrogen carbonate, in the same way as was seen in the test on page 24. This indicates the presence of carbon dioxide.

Boiling this colourless solution (⑥) will turn the solution cloudy again because calcium bicarbonate is not stable in hot water and the bicarbonate changes back into calcium carbonate, which is insoluble.

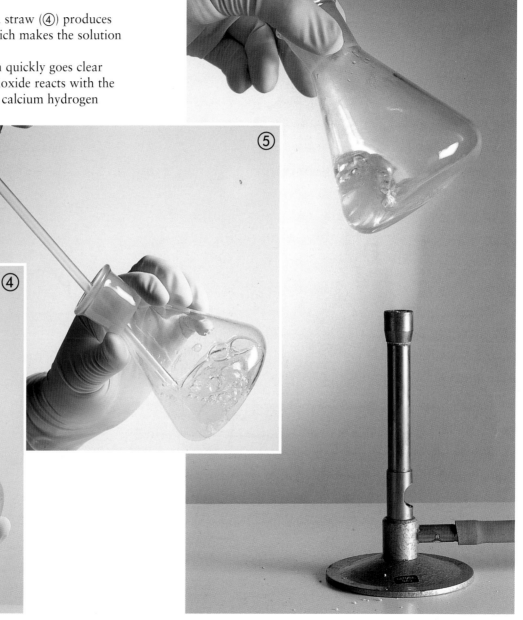

Glass straw

Limewater

25

Testing for carbon monoxide (CO)

Carbon monoxide is a colourless gas, which burns in air with a characteristic blue flame whilst being oxidised to carbon dioxide gas. Carbon monoxide is extremely poisonous and so this demonstration must be done in a fume chamber.

Unlike carbon dioxide, carbon monoxide does not affect limewater.

Demonstration: test for carbon monoxide using a lighted splint

In this demonstration, some limewater is put in the bottom of a gas jar filled with carbon monoxide (①). The limewater remains clear even when the gas jar is shaken (②).

The carbon monoxide is then ignited by inserting a lighted splint into the gas jar and leaving off the glass cover slip. The carbon monoxide burns with a characteristic blue flame (③).

As soon as the carbon monoxide stops burning and the flame goes out, the glass cover slip is replaced on the top of the gas jar to contain the gases produced by the reaction. The gas jar is shaken to mix the limewater with the gas. The limewater goes cloudy, showing that carbon dioxide is present (④) (see page 24 for an explanation of the test for carbon dioxide). When burnt, carbon monoxide reacts with the oxygen in the air to form carbon dioxide.

For this demonstration, carbon monoxide was produced by reacting concentrated sulphuric acid with sodium methanoate (sodium formate) using a dropper funnel and a conical flask and was collected over water (⑤).

PROPERTIES OF CARBON MONOXIDE

Carbon monoxide is a colourless gas with no smell. It will burn with a blue flame. Carbon monoxide is extremely toxic, competing with oxygen to be carried by haemoglobin in the blood-stream and forming compounds that block further oxygen uptake. Thus, when people breathe in carbon monoxide, they are deprived of the oxygen they need. It may affect alertness and, at concentrations of 10% of the air by volume, it is fatal within a few minutes.

Carbon monoxide has about the same density as air and is almost insoluble in water at room temperature. It is readily oxidised.

Carbon monoxide is produced during the combustion of carbon or carbon compounds in a restricted oxygen (air) supply. (Complete combustion would oxidise the carbon or carbon compounds to carbon dioxide.) For example, a typical combustion engine can produce about a tenth of its exhaust gases as carbon monoxide.

Carbon monoxide is a useful reducing agent and is used to reduce metal compounds, such as iron oxide, to the pure metal.

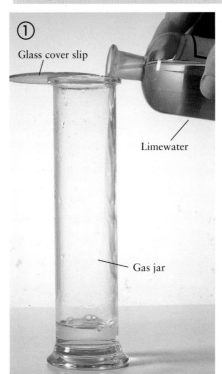

① Glass cover slip

Limewater

Gas jar

②

EQUATION: Combustion of carbon monoxide in air

Carbon monoxide + oxygen in the air ⇨ carbon dioxide

$$2CO(g) + O_2(g) \Rightarrow 2CO_2(g)$$

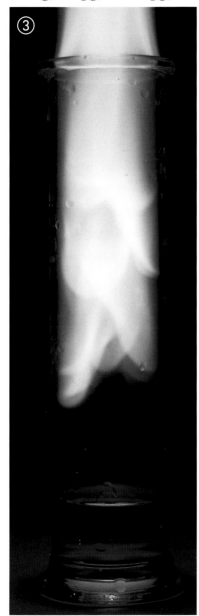

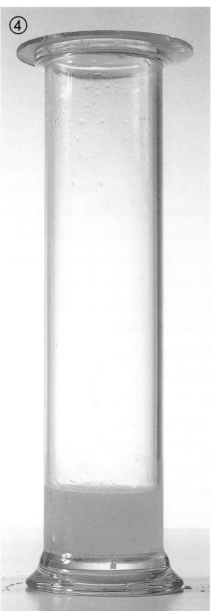

Carbon monoxide

Sulphuric acid

Sodium methanoate

(Below) In this demonstration, carbon monoxide is being used to reduce copper oxide to copper metal. At first, the carbon monoxide reacted with the oxygen in the oxide to produce carbon dioxide. As a result, the gas leaving the reduction tube does not ignite. Once reduction is complete, the carbon monoxide passes right through the tube unchanged and it is detected because it burns with a characteristic blue flame.

Testing for sulphur dioxide (SO_2)

Sulphur dioxide is a colourless, acidic gas. It is also a powerful reducing agent, and it is this property that is the basis of the tests shown here. Sulphur dioxide is poisonous and so these demonstrations are done in a fume chamber.

There are three convenient tests for a reducing agent shown here. These demonstrations show a standard preparation of sulphur dioxide. Sodium sulphite (a white powder) is first placed in the bottom of a side-arm boiling tube, and hydrochloric acid is added through a thistle funnel (①). The gas is bubbled through the test liquids or passed over soaked filter paper and the changes observed.

PROPERTIES OF SULPHUR DIOXIDE

Sulphur dioxide is a colourless, choking and poisonous gas which has a pungent smell. Sulphur dioxide is not flammable and will not support combustion.

Sulphur dioxide is over twice as dense as air. Sulphur dioxide is very soluble in water at room temperature forming an acidic solution of sulphurous acid (H_2SO_3).

Sulphur dioxide is a powerful reducing agent and bleach. Sulphur dioxide can be produced by heating and thereby decomposing some sulphur compounds.

As a product from the burning of fossil fuels, sulphur dioxide is an important air pollutant, contributing to acid rain. Sulphur dioxide is used widely in industry for the production of chemicals, as a bleach in foodstuffs and in laundry, and for preserving alcoholic drinks. It is also used in the manufacture of paper.

Demonstration 1: test for sulphur dioxide using potassium dichromate

This test is best done using a strip of filter paper soaked in potassium dichromate on which the dichromate appears yellow. The sulphur dioxide reduces the orange dichromate ions (CrO_7^{2-}) (②) in a potassium dichromate solution to blue chromium(III) ions (Cr^{3+}) (③). An intermediate green is often seen, which is a mixture of orange ions and blue ions. The same colour changes can be observed if sulphur dioxide is bubbled through a potassium dichromate solution in a test tube (④, ⑤ & ⑥).

Demonstration 2: test for sulphur dioxide using potassium permanganate solution

Sulphur dioxide is bubbled through the test solution of potassium permanganate which is reduced from

EQUATION: Preparation of sulphur dioxide gas from a sulphite salt

Sulphuric acid + sodium sulphite ⇨ sulphur dioxide + sodium sulphate + water
$H_2SO_4(aq) + Na_2SO_3(s)$ ⇨ $SO_2(g) + Na_2SO_4(aq) + H_2O(l)$

purple manganate(VII) to almost colourless manganese(II) (see page 19 for this test with hydrogen sulphide).

Demonstration 3: test for sulphur dioxide using bromine water

The sulphur dioxide is bubbled through the test solution of bromine water which is reduced from brown bromine Br_2 to colourless bromide ions Br^-.

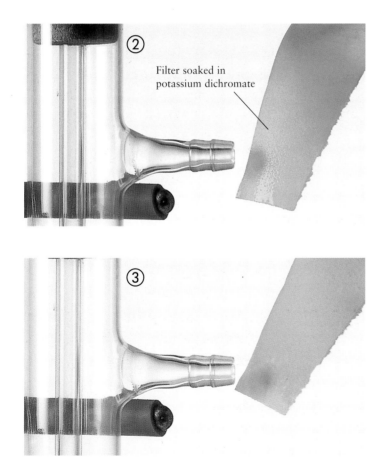

② Filter soaked in potassium dichromate

③

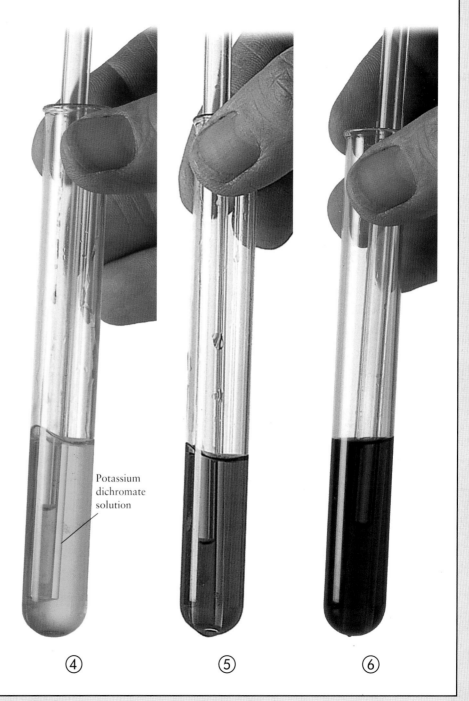

Potassium dichromate solution

④ ⑤ ⑥

Testing for hydrogen sulphide (H₂S)

Hydrogen sulphide is a colourless, acidic gas. It is extremely poisonous and so these demonstrations are done in a fume chamber. It is also a powerful reducing agent.

As a powerful reducing agent, hydrogen sulphide will change the colour of dichromate paper from orange to blue–green. It will also reduce bromine water and potassium permanganate (see page 19 for a demonstration of this with hydrogen sulphide).

However, the usual test for hydrogen sulphide is to precipitate a metal sulphide from solutions containing the metal ions. These precipitates are most often black but there are exceptions.

In these demonstrations, hydrogen sulphide is generated using a standard preparation. Iron(II) sulphide (a brown solid) is first placed in the bottom of a side-arm boiling tube, and dilute hydrochloric acid is added slowly through a thistle funnel (①).

Demonstration 1: test for hydrogen sulphide using lead acetate or lead nitrate

For this test, the gas was passed over a strip of white filter paper soaked in lead acetate solution (or lead nitrate solution) which are both colourless (②). After only a few seconds, a brown colouration can be seen on the paper (③). The lead nitrate has been converted by the hydrogen sulphide to lead

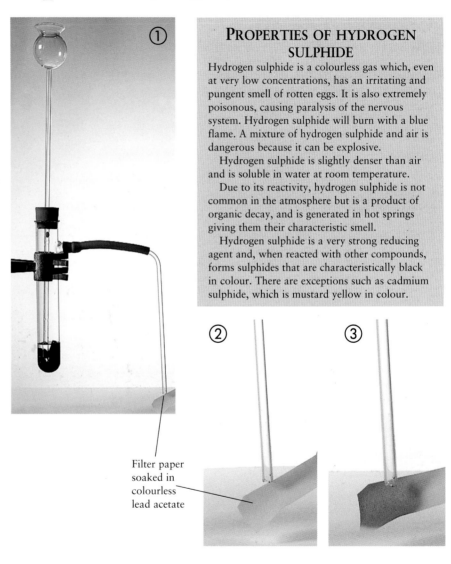

Filter paper soaked in colourless lead acetate

EQUATION: Preparation of hydrogen sulphide
Hydrochloric acid + iron(II) sulphide ⇨ *iron(II) chloride + hydrogen sulphide*
$2HCl(aq) + FeS(s) ⇨ FeCl_2(aq) + H_2S(g)$

EQUATION: **Testing for hydrogen sulphide**
Hydrogen sulphide + lead nitrate ⇨ lead sulphide + nitric acid
$H_2S(aq) + Pb(NO_3)_2(aq) \Rightarrow PbS(s) + 2HNO_3(aq)$

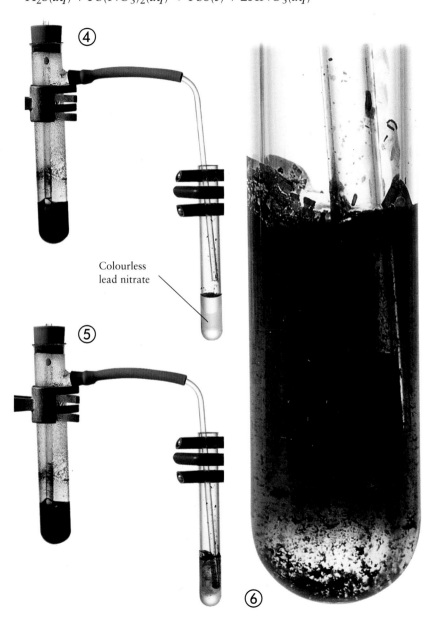

④

Colourless
lead nitrate

⑤

⑥

sulphide, which forms a black precipitate.

Bubbling the hydrogen sulphide through a test tube containing a solution of lead acetate or lead nitrate (④) shows particles of the lead sulphide precipitate (⑤).

These particles are tiny plate-like crystals which can look either black or silvery (⑥). The reason why more than one colour can be seen is that, if only small crystals of lead sulphide are produced, there is little chance for the platelets to reflect light, whereas if they are larger, the platelets will reflect the light and so look much more silvery. This is particularly noticeable if you test for hydrogen sulphide using filter paper soaked in lead nitrate because the thin film of liquid will encourage all the crystals of lead sulphide to lie flat.

Demonstration 2: test for hydrogen sulphide using cadmium sulphate

In this demonstration, hydrogen sulphide is bubbled through a colourless solution of cadmium sulphate. Immediately on reaction, a bright mustard yellow precipitate of cadmium sulphide is produced (⑦).

⑦

Testing for hydrogen chloride (HCl)

Hydrogen chloride is a colourless, acidic gas. It is harmful and corrosive and so these demonstrations are done in a fume chamber.

In these demonstrations, hydrogen chloride is generated using a standard preparation. Sodium chloride (a refined version of common salt) is first placed in the bottom of a side-arm boiling tube and concentrated sulphuric acid is added slowly through a thistle funnel (①). The hydrogen chloride gas generated may be tested.

EQUATION: Preparation of hydrogen chloride
Sodium chloride + sulphuric acid ⇨ sodium hydrogen sulphate
+ hydrogen chloride

$NaCl(s) + H_2SO_4(conc) ⇨ NaHSO_4(s) + HCl(g)$

Demonstration 1: test for hydrogen chloride by acidity

The presence of an acid gas can be detected by using a strip of filter paper soaked in Universal Indicator solution. The indicator paper turns from green (②) to yellow (③) to red (④).

The indicator only shows that an acidic gas is present. There are other acidic gases, such as sulphur dioxide, hydrogen sulphide and nitrogen dioxide; and so we need to perform more tests to determine that the gas is hydrogen chloride.

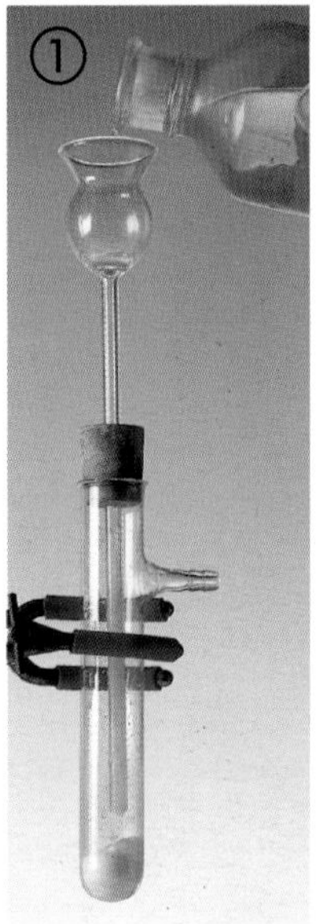

(Below) Because hydrogen chloride is very soluble, when it escapes from the side arm, it dissolves in the water. Hydrogen chloride gas molecules ionise in water, forming hydrogen ions, which are responsible for acidity. The pH of the solution will fall rapidly and the colour of the solution will change from green to yellow to red.

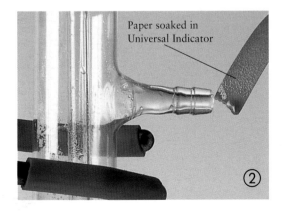

Paper soaked in Universal Indicator

②

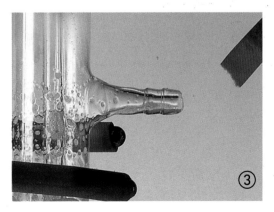

③

④

Demonstration 2: test for hydrogen chloride using silver nitrate

When hydrogen chloride is dissolved in water, it produces chloride ions (Cl^-) as well as hydrogen ions (H^+). A silver nitrate solution can be used to detect chloride ions.

In this demonstration, hydrogen chloride is bubbled through a colourless solution of silver nitrate, which has been acidified with some drops of dilute nitric acid (⑤). A precipitate of white silver chloride is produced (⑥).

A standard way of showing that we have a precipitate of silver chloride as opposed to silver bromide, which might be produced by hydrogen bromide gas (see page 36) is to dissolve the precipitate by adding ammonia solution (see page 34).

Having conducted this test, it is known that the gas is not only acidic and so produces hydrogen ions, but that the gas also produces chloride ions. There are very few colourless gases which produce both of these ions, and hydrogen chloride is the most likely common gas.

Demonstration 3: test for hydrogen chloride using ammonia solution

An alternative common test is to react the hydrogen chloride with ammonia. In this demonstration, a strip of filter paper soaked in concentrated ammonia is held in the gas stream (⑦). The reaction produces a distinctive white smoke of ammonium chloride (see page 34).

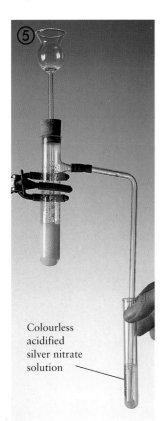

Colourless
acidified
silver nitrate
solution

PROPERTIES OF HYDROGEN CHLORIDE

Hydrogen chloride gas is colourless, and pungent smelling. However, if any of the gas is inhaled, it produces immediate, severe irritation of the nose and throat because it dissolves in the mucous membranes and immediately turns into hydrochloric acid.

Hydrogen chloride is a little denser than air. Hydrogen chloride is very soluble in water at room temperature and produces a solution of hydrochloric acid.

Hydrogen chloride is rare in nature, occurring around the vents of active volcanoes.

Testing for ammonia (NH₃)

Ammonia is colourless and is the only common alkaline gas. Because ammonia has a pungent smell, these demonstrations are done in a fume chamber.

In these demonstrations, ammonia is generated using a standard preparation. Ammonium sulphate (a white powder) is first placed in the bottom of a side-arm boiling tube, and hot sodium hydroxide solution is added slowly through a thistle funnel. The ammonia gas generated can be tested.

Demonstration 1: test for ammonia by acidity

If wet litmus paper is exposed to ammonia gas (①), it will turn blue (②) showing that the gas present is alkaline. Because ammonia is the only common alkaline gas, this is almost always a sufficient test.

Demonstration 2: test for ammonia using hydrochloric acid (hydrogen chloride solution)

A strip of filter paper is soaked in concentrated hydrochloric acid and exposed to ammonia gas (③). A white smoke, consisting of fine ammonium chloride particles, is produced.

①

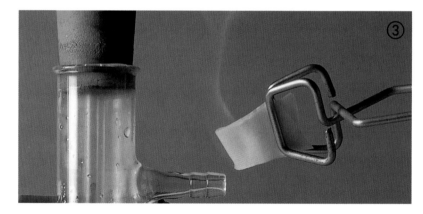
②

③

PROPERTIES OF AMMONIA

Ammonia is colourless and has a pungent smell, which is choking when inhaled but not poisonous. Ammonium carbonate crystals are used as 'smelling salts'. Ammonia is not flammable in air but will combine with oxygen gas.

Ammonia is much less dense than air. Ammonia is extremely soluble in water producing an alkaline solution. Ammonia is the only common 'alkaline' gas.

EQUATION: Preparing ammonia in the laboratory

Ammonium sulphate + calcium hydroxide ⇨ ammonia + water + calcium sulphate

$(NH_4)_2SO_4(s) + Ca(OH)_2(s) ⇨ 2NH_3(g) + 2H_2O(l) + CaSO_4(s)$

EQUATION: Testing for ammonia in the laboratory

Concentrated hydrochloric acid + ammonia ⇨ ammonium chloride

$HCl(conc) + NH_3(g) ⇨ NH_4Cl(s)$

Testing for nitrogen monoxide (NO)

Nitrogen monoxide is a neutral, colourless gas. It is poisonous and so these demonstrations are done in a fume chamber.

Demonstration: test for nitrogen monoxide using air

In this demonstration, nitrogen monoxide is generated using a standard preparation. Copper turnings are first placed in the bottom of a side-arm boiling tube, and dilute nitric acid is then added slowly through a thistle funnel (①).

The nitrogen monoxide gas in the side-arm boiling tube and delivery tube is colourless (②) but, as it emerges from the end of a delivery tube, it reacts with oxygen in the air to produce nitrogen dioxide, which is a brown gas (③). Nitrogen monoxide is the only gas that will do this and so a colour change is normally an adequate test.

You can distinguish between nitrogen monoxide and oxygen, another common colourless gas, because nitrogen monoxide will not relight a glowing splint.

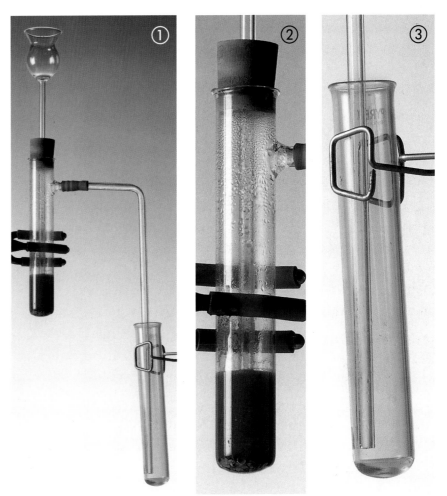

EQUATION: Preparation of nitrogen monoxide
Dilute nitric acid + copper ⇨ copper(II) nitrate + nitrogen monoxide + water
$8HNO_3(aq) + 3Cu(s) ⇨ 3Cu(NO_3)_2(aq) + 2NO(g) + 4H_2O(l)$

EQUATION: Reaction of nitrogen monoxide and oxygen
Nitrogen monoxide+ oxygen ⇨ nitrogen dioxide
$2NO(g) + O_2(g) ⇨ 2NO_2(g)$

Testing for hydrogen bromide (HBr)

Hydrogen bromide is a colourless, fuming, acidic gas. It is poisonous and so these demonstrations are done in a fume chamber.

Demonstration: test for hydrogen bromide

In this demonstration, hydrogen bromide is generated using a standard preparation. Potassium bromide (a white powder) is first placed in the bottom of a side-arm boiling tube, and concentrated sulphuric acid is added slowly through a thistle funnel. The gas generated may be observed (because the 'fumes' are visible in moist air) and tested (①).

Although hydrogen bromide is colourless, it is almost always released together with brown bromine gas.

The presence of an acid gas can be detected by using a strip of (green) wetted pH paper which rapidly turns red. The effect of the bromine gas that is also present would bleach the paper in time (see page 37 opposite) but the combination of hydrogen bromide and bromine is so corrosive that it quickly destroys the end of the paper (②).

In this test, the presence of brown bromine vapour also indicates that the acidic gas is probably hydrogen bromide.

EQUATION: Preparation of hydrogen bromide

Potassium bromide + concentrated sulphuric acid ⇨ potassium sulphate + hydrogen bromide

$2KBr(s) + H_2SO_4(conc) ⇨ K_2SO_4(aq) + 2HBr(g)$

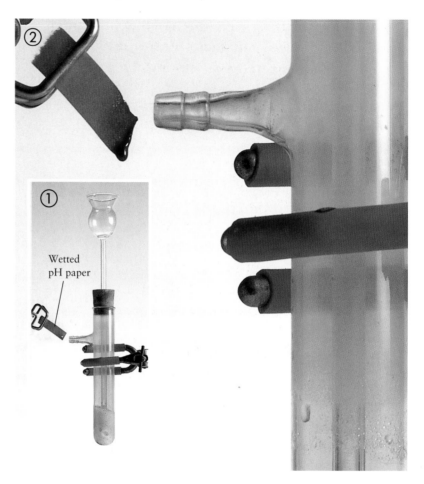

Wetted pH paper

PROPERTIES OF HYDROGEN BROMIDE

Hydrogen bromide gas is colourless and pungent smelling. However, if any of the gas is inhaled, it produces immediate, severe irritation of the nose and throat because it dissolves in the mucous membranes and immediately turns into the strongly acidic hydrobromic acid.

Hydrogen bromide is nearly three times denser than air. Hydrogen bromide is very soluble in water at room temperature, and it will react directly with moisture in the air, producing fumes of hydrobromic acid.

Testing for bromine (Br$_2$)

Bromine is a brown gas. It is acidic, a powerful oxidising agent and a bleach. It is very poisonous and so these demonstrations are done in a fume chamber.

Demonstration: test for bromine

Bromine is a liquid at room temperature. To obtain the gas, a small amount of liquid is warmed in the bottom of a side-arm boiling tube. This produces the required vapour (①), which can be observed and tested.

The bromine vapour reacts with wetted (green) pH paper (②) to form an acidic solution that turns the paper dull red (③). As it changes colour, the paper is bleached very rapidly (④).

The only other common brown gas is nitrogen dioxide. Nitrogen dioxide produces a much more acidic reaction before bleaching pH paper and turns the paper bright red before bleaching it slowly (see page 36). Bromine tends to produce only a dull red colouration to pH paper because bleaching takes place so rapidly.

Furthermore, if bromine gas is bubbled into water, it produces a light brown solution, whereas nitrogen dioxide gas bubbled into water produces a colourless solution (see page 40 for this comparison).

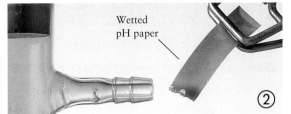

Wetted pH paper

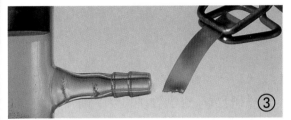

PROPERTIES OF BROMINE

Bromine gas is a brown, pungent-smelling gas. The word bromine comes from the Greek *bromos*, meaning stench. Bromine irritates the membranes of the nose at very low concentrations, and at only slightly higher concentrations it causes difficulty in breathing.

Bromine is almost five and a half times denser than air. Bromine is slightly soluble in water at room temperature but is very soluble in organic solvents (see page 49).

Bromine gas is highly reactive, forming compounds, and so is never found naturally in its elemental state. It can be found in sea water and in rocks. Bromine is a powerful oxidising agent.

Testing for nitrogen dioxide (NO_2)

Nitrogen dioxide is a brown gas. It is acidic, a powerful oxidising agent and a bleach. Nitrogen dioxide is very poisonous and so these demonstrations are done in a fume chamber.

Demonstration: test for nitrogen dioxide

In this demonstration, nitrogen dioxide is generated using a standard method of preparation (①). Copper turnings are first placed in the bottom of a side-arm boiling tube, and concentrated nitric acid is added slowly through a thistle funnel. The nitrogen dioxide generated can be observed and tested.

The nitrogen dioxide is acidic and so turns wetted (green) pH paper (②) red (③). The paper is then bleached by the nitrogen dioxide.

Nitrogen dioxide is also distinctively reddish-brown and denser than air. The only other common brown gas is bromine, and therefore identification is to distinguish between bromine and nitrogen dioxide. Nitrogen dioxide produces a much more acidic reaction before bleaching pH paper and turns the paper bright red before bleaching it slowly. The bromine tends to produce only a dull red colouration to pH paper because bleaching takes place so rapidly (see page 36). Furthermore, if nitrogen dioxide is bubbled into water, it does not colour the solution, whereas bromine gas bubbled into water produces a brown colour in the solution (see page 40 for this comparison).

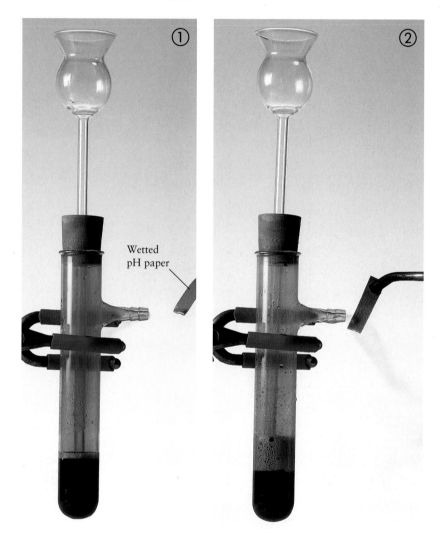

Wetted
pH paper

EQUATION: Preparation of nitrogen dioxide
Copper + nitric acid ⇨ nitrogen dioxide + copper(II) nitrate + water
$Cu(s) + 4HNO_3(conc) ⇨ 2NO_2(g) + Cu(NO_3)_2(aq) + 2H_2O(l)$

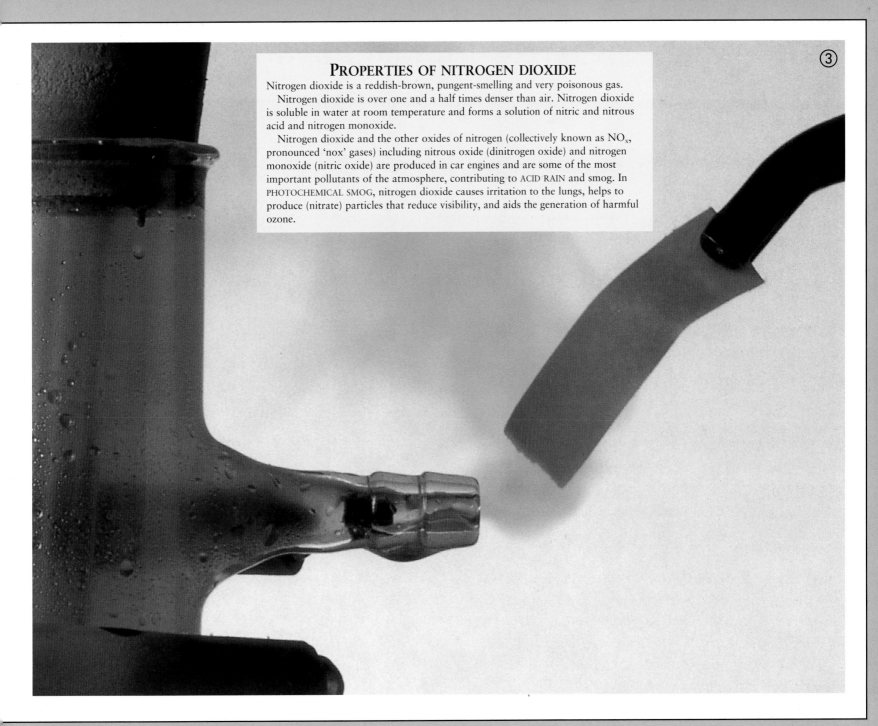

PROPERTIES OF NITROGEN DIOXIDE

③

Nitrogen dioxide is a reddish-brown, pungent-smelling and very poisonous gas.

Nitrogen dioxide is over one and a half times denser than air. Nitrogen dioxide is soluble in water at room temperature and forms a solution of nitric and nitrous acid and nitrogen monoxide.

Nitrogen dioxide and the other oxides of nitrogen (collectively known as NO_x, pronounced 'nox' gases) including nitrous oxide (dinitrogen oxide) and nitrogen monoxide (nitric oxide) are produced in car engines and are some of the most important pollutants of the atmosphere, contributing to ACID RAIN and smog. In PHOTOCHEMICAL SMOG, nitrogen dioxide causes irritation to the lungs, helps to produce (nitrate) particles that reduce visibility, and aids the generation of harmful ozone.

Distinguishing between bromine and nitrogen dioxide

Bromine gas (see page 37) and nitrogen dioxide (see pages 38 and 39) are both brown gases. They are both acidic and both bleach indicator paper. Although the rate at which the indicator paper turns red and is bleached can be used to distinguish between the gases, this method is not precise. However, bromine will colour water brown and nitrogen dioxide will not.

Demonstration: distinguishing between bromine and nitrogen dioxide

In this demonstration, bromine is bubbled through water (①) and colours it brown (②). In contrast, if nitrogen dioxide is bubbled through water (③), the liquid remains colourless (④).

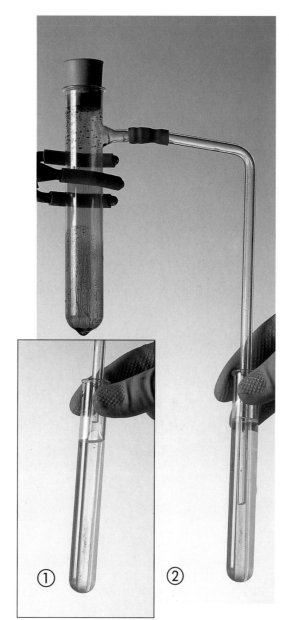

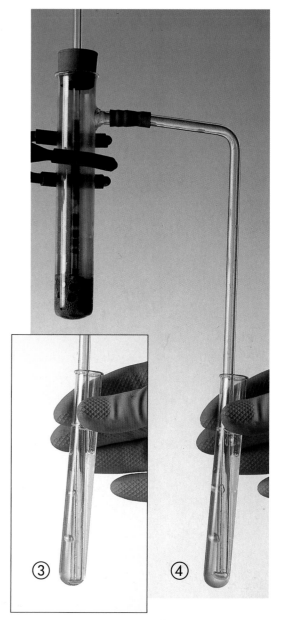

Testing for iodine vapour (I$_2$)

Iodine has a characteristic violet colour. Iodine is acidic, an oxidising agent and a bleach. Iodine is very poisonous and so these demonstrations are done in a fume chamber.

Demonstration: test for iodine vapour using pH paper

Iodine vapour is prepared by adding concentrated sulphuric acid through a thistle funnel to potassium iodide in a side-arm boiling tube. The heat of the reaction vaporises the iodine. This produces the required vapour, which can be observed and tested.

Iodine reacts with water to form an acidic solution, which will turn wetted (green) pH paper red. Iodine is also an oxidising agent and it bleaches the pH paper white as well as condensing on the paper as a violet-coloured deposit (①). Because iodine is an oxidising agent, the pH paper bleaches as it changes colour, so the colour seen is only a pale red.

Remarks

Iodine is not very soluble in water, but is extremely soluble in organic solvents. If iodine is bubbled into a mixture of water and an organic solvent like methylbenzene, the iodine will dissolve in the layer of methylbenzene giving it a strong violet colour, whilst the water will be a pale brown layer where the iodine has barely dissolved.

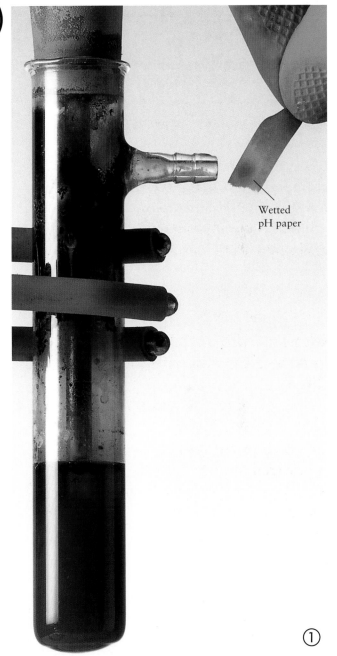

Wetted
pH paper

①

PROPERTIES OF IODINE

Iodine gas is a violet, pungent-smelling gas. The word iodine comes from the Greek *iodes*, meaning violet. Iodine irritates the membranes of the nose at very low concentrations and, at only slightly higher concentrations, it causes difficulty in breathing.

Iodine is almost nine times denser than air. Iodine is only slightly soluble in water at room temperature but is very soluble in organic solvents (see page 49).

Iodine gas is highly reactive forming compounds and so is never found naturally in its elemental state. It can be found in sea water and in rocks. Iodine is an oxidising agent.

Testing for chlorine (Cl_2)

Chlorine is a characteristically greenish-yellow gas (①). It is acidic, a powerful oxidising agent and a bleach. Chlorine is very poisonous and so these demonstrations are done in a fume chamber.

In these demonstrations, chlorine is generated using a standard method of preparation (②). Sodium chlorate(I) solution is first placed in the bottom of a side-arm boiling tube and hydrochloric acid is added slowly through a thistle funnel. The chlorine gas generated can be tested.

Demonstration 1: test for chlorine by acidity and bleaching

If indicators are exposed to chlorine, they will show it to be an acid gas. Damp litmus will turn pink and damp green pH paper (③) will turn red (④). In both cases, the paper will then be quickly bleached (⑤). It is this rapid bleaching that distinguishes chlorine from many other acid gases such as sulphur dioxide, hydrogen sulphide and nitrogen dioxide.

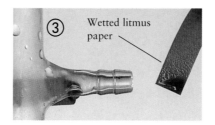

Wetted litmus paper

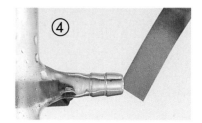

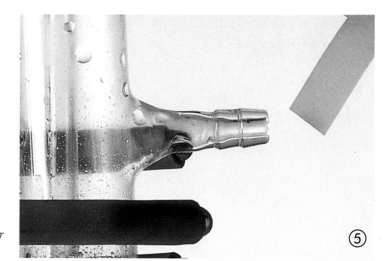

EQUATION: Preparation of chlorine
Hydrochloric acid + sodium chlorate(I) ⇨ chlorine + sodium chloride + water
$2HCl(aq) + NaOCl(aq) ⇨ Cl_2(g) + 2NaCl(aq) + H_2O(l)$

Demonstration 2: test for chlorine with potassium iodide

Chlorine is a powerful oxidising agent. Chlorine will, for example, oxidise colourless iodide ions to iodine atoms and molecules which are brown. This can be seen when chlorine is passed over filter paper that is soaked in potassium iodide solution (⑥ & ⑦). Alternatively, chlorine can be bubbled through potassium iodide solution to see the change from colourless to brown solution (⑧, ⑨ & ⑩).

Demonstration 3: test for chlorine with starch–iodide

Damp starch–iodide paper turns blue–black in the presence of chlorine.

PROPERTIES OF CHLORINE

Chlorine gas is greenish-yellow and has a pungent smell. Chlorine irritates the membranes of the nose at very low concentrations and, at only slightly higher concentrations, it causes difficulty in breathing. A flame will continue to burn in chlorine.

Chlorine has almost two and a half times the density of air. Chlorine is slightly soluble in water at room temperature forming hydrochloric (HCl) and hypochlorous (HOCl) acids. Chlorine is very soluble in organic solvents (see page 49).

Chlorine gas is highly reactive, forming compounds, and so is never found naturally in its elemental state. It can be found as sodium chloride in sea water and in rocks. Chlorine is a powerful oxidising agent.

⑧   ⑨   ⑩

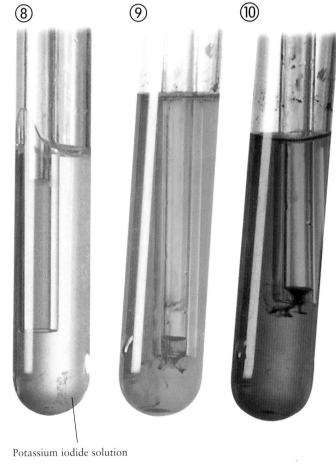

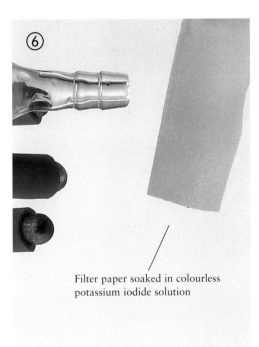

Filter paper soaked in colourless potassium iodide solution

Potassium iodide solution

43

FLAME TESTS

Flame tests are a quick and simple, but not very accurate, method for indicating the presence of certain metal ions in substances.

Demonstration: conducting a flame test

A rod or wire is dipped into the compound being tested and then placed in a Bunsen flame. A solution or suspension in concentrated hydrochloric acid often gives a stronger colouration.

Some of the most common flame colours are shown here. However, only those metal ions that emit light in the visible spectrum can be tested by this method.

NOTE: A much more sophisticated flame test used in research laboratories is atomic emission spectroscopy, which detects all of the characteristic radiation from a metal, including that which cannot be seen because it is outside the visible spectrum. It also allows very small amounts of metal ions to be measured (e.g. sodium ions in blood samples).

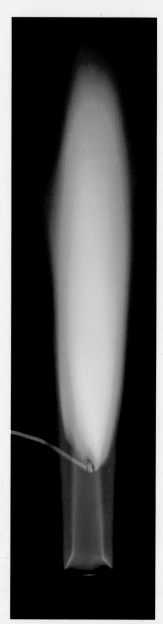

Intense yellow-coloured sodium flame

Lilac-coloured potassium flame

Brick-red calcium flame

Red strontium flame

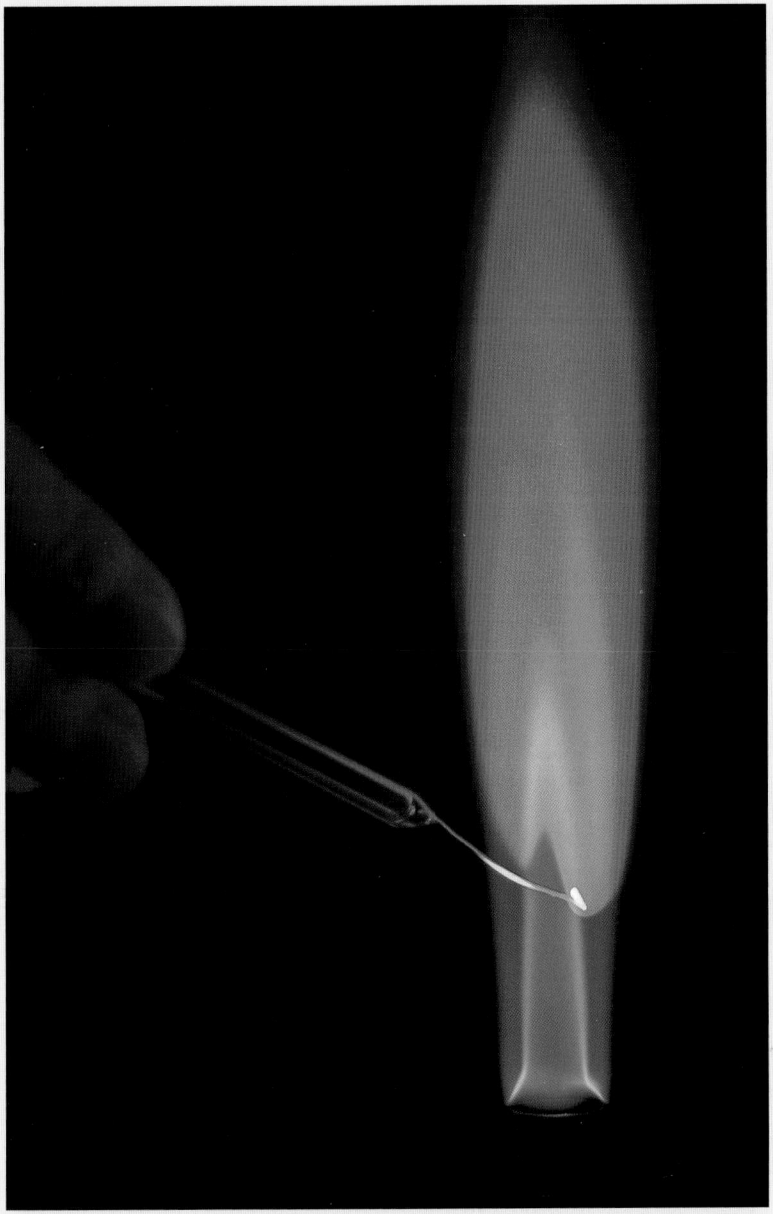

Green–blue
copper flame

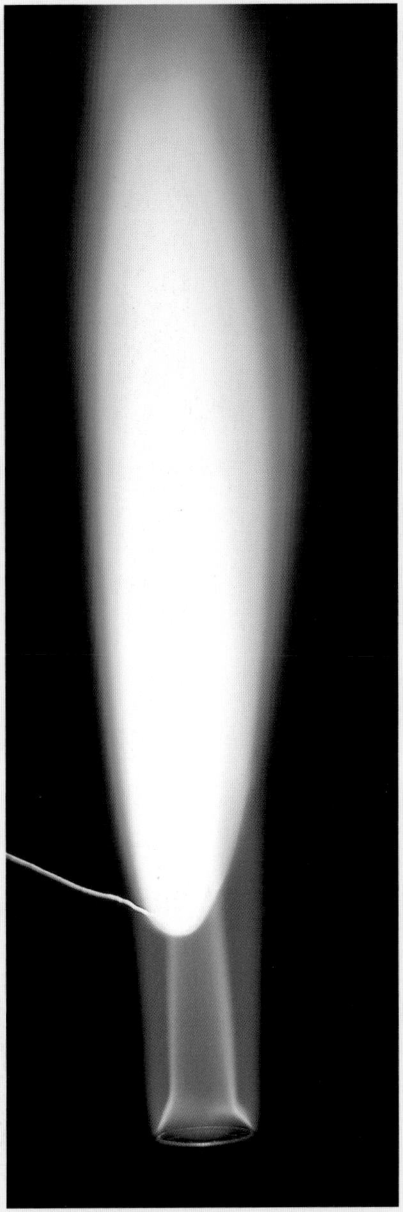

Brown–green
barium flame

TESTING FOR IONS IN SOLUTION

What are ions?

An ATOM is the smallest particle of an element, which shows its chemical properties. An atom is made up of a NUCLEUS and its surrounding ELECTRONS. Atoms have no electrical charge but this does not mean they are stable. They may lose or gain electrons. If an atom, or group of atoms has lost or gained one or more electrons, they become charged particles or ions. Ions are either positively charged, in which case they are called CATIONS, or negatively charged, in which case they are called ANIONS.

Sodium atoms (Na), for example, lose one electron when they react to reach a more stable state. In so doing, sodium ions (Na^+) are formed with an overall positive charge (cations) equivalent to one electron. Chlorine atoms (Cl), in contrast, become more stable if they each gain one electron and become chloride ions (Cl^-) with an overall negative charge equivalent to one electron.

If a compound contains ions, it is described as ionic. Ionic compounds are held together by the attracting of the opposing charges of the anions and cations present. Sodium chloride (NaCl – common salt) is an example of an ionic compound.

Ionic compounds may be found as rigid, crystalline solids such as rock salt. However, if the solid is dissolved to form a solution, the ions become free to move. Salt can be dissolved in water to give such a solution.

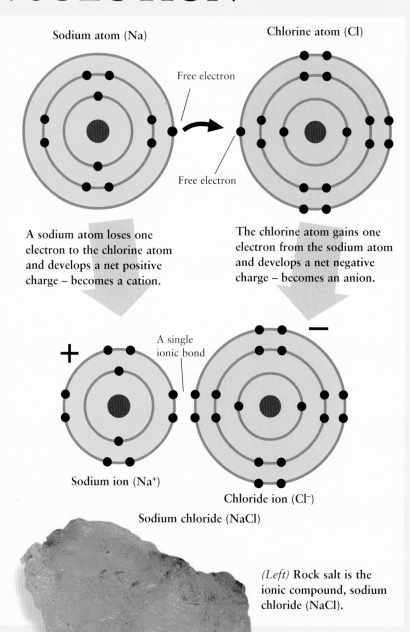

Sodium atom (Na)

Chlorine atom (Cl)

Free electron

Free electron

A sodium atom loses one electron to the chlorine atom and develops a net positive charge – becomes a cation.

The chlorine atom gains one electron from the sodium atom and develops a net negative charge – becomes an anion.

A single ionic bond

Sodium ion (Na^+)

Chloride ion (Cl^-)

Sodium chloride (NaCl)

(Left) Rock salt is the ionic compound, sodium chloride (NaCl).

In solution, the separated ions become attached to molecules of the solvent by strong forces of electrical attraction. A solution containing a large number of ions, such as sodium chloride dissolved in water, conducts electricity well – it is an electrolyte. Ions play the same role of conducting electricity in a solution as electrons do in conducting electricity in a solid.

Detecting ions

Ions in solution are free to move about and so they can easily react with new ions introduced into the solution. In some cases, the forces of attraction between the new groupings of ions will be sufficiently strong to make a new compound that is a solid. This is seen as a precipitate in the solution. These new precipitates may have characteristic colours and may appear granular or gelatinous. The precipitates may also redissolve if other substances are added. This can be used as a test, because, as we know which chemicals we have added, we can then find out which ions were present in the original solution.

For example, if silver nitrate is added to a solution containing chloride ions, a characteristic white, granular precipitate of silver chloride is produced. This silver chloride can be redissolved if ammonia solution is added.

Sometimes a test requires more than one stage.

The chart opposite shows the tests for some common anions and cations. They are all demonstrated in the last part of this book.

SUMMARY OF TESTS FOR IONS IN SOLUTION

ANIONS (pages 46 to 56)

Chloride (Cl^-): Add a small amount of dilute nitric acid and then a small amount of silver nitrate solution. If chloride ions are present, this produces a white precipitate of silver chloride which is soluble in ammonia solution.

Bromide (Br^-): Add a small amount of dilute nitric acid and then a small amount of silver nitrate solution. If bromide ions are present, this produces a pale yellow precipitate of silver bromide which is slightly soluble in ammonia solution.

Iodide (I^-): Add a small amount of dilute nitric acid and then a small amount of silver nitrate solution. If iodide ions are present, this produces a yellow precipitate of silver iodide. It is insoluble in ammonia solution.

Sulphide (S^{2-}): Add dilute hydrochloric acid. If sulphide ions are present, hydrogen sulphide gas will be produced which can be tested with filter paper soaked in lead nitrate solution, turning it black.

Sulphate (SO_4^{2-}): Add a small amount of barium chloride solution and then a small amount of dilute hydrochloric acid. If sulphate ions are present, this produces a white precipitate of barium sulphate.

Nitrate (NO_3^-): Make the solution strongly alkaline. Add Devarda's alloy and warm. If nitrate ions are present, this produces ammonia gas which can be tested with filter paper dipped in hydrochloric acid.

Carbonate (CO_3^{2-}): Add dilute hydrochloric acid to the solution. Bubbles of carbon dioxide are given off.

CATIONS (pages 57 to 65)

Ammonium (NH_4^+): Add sodium hydroxide solution and heat gently. Ammonia is given off.

Aluminium (Al^{3+}): Add sodium hydroxide solution and a colourless, gelatinous precipitate of aluminium hydroxide forms that dissolves in excess hydroxide. Adding ammonia solution will produce the same precipitate but not redissolve it.

Copper (Cu^{2+}): Add sodium hydroxide solution and a blue gelatinous precipitate of copper(II) hydroxide forms. Add ammonia solution and the precipitate dissolves to give a deep blue solution.

Iron(II) (Fe^{2+}): Add sodium hydroxide solution and a yellow–green gelatinous precipitate of iron(II) hydroxide forms.

Iron(III) (Fe^{3+}): Add sodium hydroxide solution and a reddish–brown gelatinous precipitate of iron(III) hydroxide forms.

Lead(II) (Pb^{2+}): Add sodium hydroxide solution and a white, granular precipitate of lead(II) hydroxide forms, which then dissolves in excess hydroxide. The precipitate does not dissolve in ammonia solution.

Zinc (Zn^{2+}): Add sodium hydroxide solution and a white, gelatinous precipitate of zinc hydroxide forms which dissolves in excess hydroxide. The precipitate dissolves in excess ammonia.

Testing for chloride (Cl⁻), bromide (Br⁻) and iodide (I⁻)

Chloride, bromide and iodide are the common HALIDE ions. Halide ions (anions) can be found in many substances, from common salt in sea water, to a common laboratory reagent potassium iodide solution.

Halides react with silver ions to form precipitates with various colours and with varying tendencies to redissolve in ammonia solution.

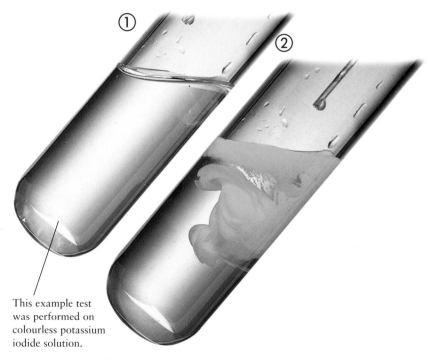

This example test was performed on colourless potassium iodide solution.

EQUATION: **Example: test for an iodide**
Potassium iodide + lead(II) nitrate ⇨ lead(II) iodide + potassium nitrate
$2KI(aq) + Pb(NO_3)_2(aq) ⇨ PbI_2(s) + 2KNO_3(aq)$

Demonstration 1: testing for halides using silver nitrate

To test for halide ions, (colourless) dilute nitric acid and (colourless) silver nitrate solution (①) are added to the test solution. Any precipitate (②) indicates the presence of halide ions.

If iodide ions are present, the precipitate is <u>yellow</u> silver iodide (②).

If, however, chloride ions are present, a <u>white</u> precipitate of silver chloride will form (see opposite page).

If bromide ions are present, a pale yellow precipitate of silver bromide will form (see page 49).

Demonstration 2: Comparing the halides using ammonia solution

In this test, a few drops of dilute nitric acid and silver nitrate solution are placed in each of three tubes. To this, sodium chloride (left), sodium bromide (centre), and sodium iodide (right) are added with a pipette (③).

This produces white, pale yellow and yellow precipitates, showing there are chloride ions, bromide ions and iodide ions in the tubes, respectively.

Because the colours are not always easy to tell apart, a further test can now be performed using ammonia. If concentrated ammonia solution (④) is added, the 'chloride' tube changes to a clear, colourless solution, the 'bromide' tube becomes slightly clearer, but there is no change in the 'iodide' tube.

Remarks

Further tests can be performed if needed. If the precipitate is silver chloride, the addition of concentrated sulphuric acid will produce steamy fumes of hydrogen chloride gas (see page 32 for tests for hydrogen chloride gas).

If the precipitate is silver bromide, addition of concentrated sulphuric acid will produce steamy fumes of hydrogen bromide and brown bromine (see pages 36 and 37 for tests for hydrogen bromide gas and bromine gas, respectively).

Demonstration 3: solubility of halogens using an organic solvent

Halogens dissolve far better in organic solvents than they do in water. If methylbenzene is poured on to water in a test tube and, from left to right, iodine, bromine and chlorine added, the colours in the methylbenzene are violet for iodine, brown for bromine and green for chlorine (⑤).

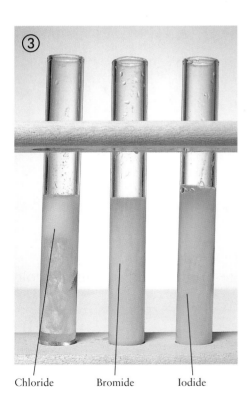

③

Chloride   Bromide   Iodide

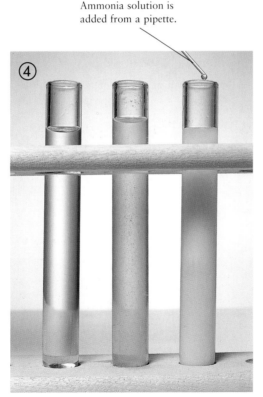

④

Ammonia solution is added from a pipette.

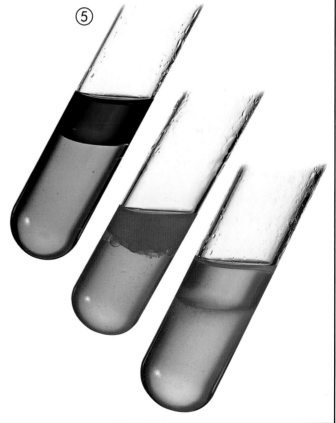

⑤

Testing for sulphide (S^{2-}) ions

The sulphide ion is an anion of sulphur only and is a weak ACID RADICAL. Common sulphides include iron(II) sulphide, zinc sulphide, sodium sulphide and copper(II) sulphide.

Demonstration: test for sulphide by reaction with an acid

Sulphides, sulphites, carbonates and nitrites will evolve gas when reacted with an acid. The test is therefore to distinguish between these gases. In the case of a sulphide, hydrogen sulphide is produced and can be tested for.

Hydrogen sulphide is very poisonous (and pungent smelling) so this test is done in a fume chamber. Dilute hydrochloric acid is added to the white powder suspected to contain a sulphide (①). The powder in this demonstration is sodium sulphide.

The hydrogen sulphide which is produced can be tested for using a strip of filter paper soaked in lead nitrate solution. The reaction changes the colourless lead nitrate solution (②), precipitating lead sulphide to give a grey or black colouration to the paper (③ & ④).

Other tests for hydrogen sulphide are shown on page 30.

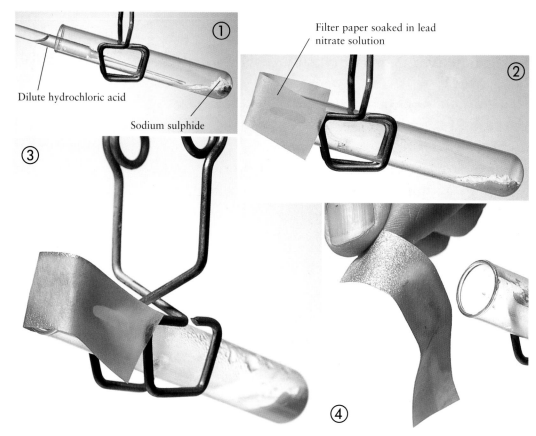

Dilute hydrochloric acid

Sodium sulphide

Filter paper soaked in lead nitrate solution

①

②

③

④

EQUATION: Test for a sulphide – reaction with an acid produces hydrogen sulphide
Hydrochloric acid + sodium sulphide ⇨ hydrogen sulphide + sodium chloride
$2HCl(aq) + Na_2S(s) \Rightarrow H_2S(g) + 2NaCl(aq)$

IONIC EQUATION: Test for a sulphide
Hydrogen ions + sulphide ions ⇨ hydrogen sulphide gas
$2H^+(aq) + S^{2-}(aq) \Rightarrow H_2S(g)$

Testing for sulphate (SO_4^{2-}) ions

Common sulphates include sodium sulphate, copper(II) sulphate and barium sulphate.

Demonstration: test for sulphate using a barium salt

In this test the solution suspected of containing sulphate ions is dropped into a boiling tube containing colourless solution of barium nitrate and excess nitric acid or hydrochloric acid (①). A white, granular precipitate of barium sulphate forms (②). In this demonstration, the solution being tested was colourless sodium sulphate.

Here the use of barium ions is significant. There are remarkably few insoluble salts of barium which can exist in the presence of the mineral acids, hydrochloric or nitric acid. The salt, barium sulphate, is the exception and so the production of a precipitate from barium ions in the presence of hydrochloric acid or nitric acid is a specific test for sulphate ions.

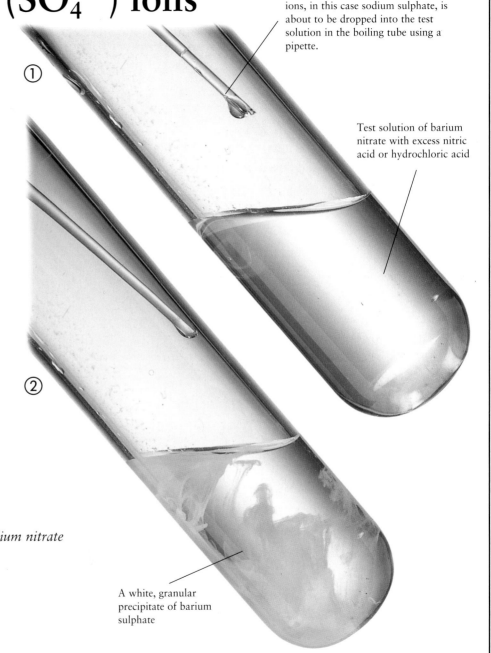

Suspected solution containing sulphate ions, in this case sodium sulphate, is about to be dropped into the test solution in the boiling tube using a pipette.

Test solution of barium nitrate with excess nitric acid or hydrochloric acid

A white, granular precipitate of barium sulphate

EQUATION: **Test for a sulphate**
Sodium sulphate + barium nitrate ⇨ barium sulphate + sodium nitrate
$Na_2SO_4(aq) + Ba(NO_3)_2(aq) \Rightarrow BaSO_4(s) + 2NaNO_3(aq)$

IONIC EQUATION: **Test for a sulphate**
Sulphate ions + nitrate ions ⇨ barium sulphate solid
$SO_4^{2-}(aq) + Ba^{2+}(aq) \Rightarrow BaSO_4(s)$

Testing for nitrate (NO$_3^-$) ions

The nitrate ion is an anion of nitrogen and oxygen. Common nitrates include potassium nitrate, sodium nitrate, calcium nitrate and barium nitrate.

Demonstration 1: test using DEVARDA'S ALLOY (a mixture of zinc and copper metal granules)

This test has two stages and identifies the presence of nitrate ions through the production of ammonia gas.

The first stage is concerned with showing that the ammonium ion (NH$_4^+$) is not present in the substance under test.

Solid nitrate is placed in a boiling tube and sodium hydroxide solution is added to make a strongly alkaline solution (①). This solution is then heated (②). When wetted pH paper is held in front of the mouth of the tube, it shows no colour change (③), showing that there is no ammonia given off and, by deduction, no ammonium ions (NH$_4^+$) in the original compound. If ammonium ions had been present and ammonia gas given off, it would have been necessary to boil the solution until no more ammonia gas was evolved (i.e. all ammonium ions destroyed) before the next stage of the test was done.

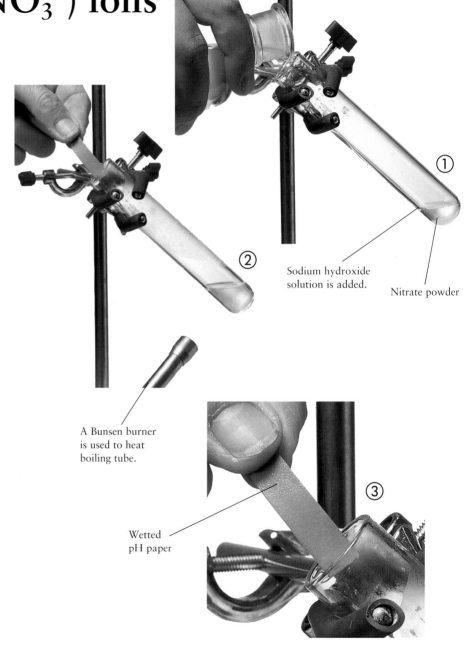

①

②

Sodium hydroxide solution is added.

Nitrate powder

A Bunsen burner is used to heat boiling tube.

③

Wetted pH paper

In the second stage, some Devarda's alloy is added to the solution (④). Devarda's alloy reacts with the sodium hydroxide, acting as a strong reducing agent (⑤), reducing the nitrate ions and releasing ammonia. The damp pH paper turns blue (⑥) indicating an alkaline gas is present which is a positive test for ammonia (see page 34 for more on ammonia gas).

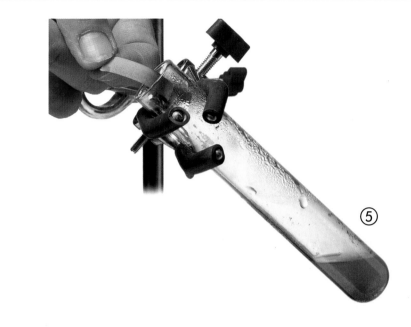

④ Devarda's alloy is added with a spatula.

EQUATION: Test for a nitrate – reaction with an acid

Zinc + sodium nitrate + sodium hydroxide ⇨ sodium zincate + ammonia + water

$4Zn(s) + NaNO_3(s) + 7NaOH(aq) ⇨ 4Na_2ZnO_2 + NH_3(g) + 2H_2O(aq)$

IONIC EQUATION: Test for a nitrate

Zinc + hydroxide ions + nitrate ions ⇨ ammonia gas + zincate ions + hydroxide ions + water

$4Zn(s) + 7OH^-(aq) + NO_3^-(s) ⇨ NH_3(g) + 4ZnO_2^{2-}(aq) + 2H_2O(aq)$

Demonstration 2: the brown ring test for nitrates

In this test, an aqueous solution of dilute sulphuric acid and iron(II) sulphate are added to a boiling tube containing the sample of suspected nitrate (①).

Concentrated sulphuric acid is slowly poured into the tube and because it is more dense than the nitrate it will form a layer underneath the nitrate (②). A brown layer (ring) develops at the junction between the two liquids (③ & ④). The presence of the brown ring confirms the presence of a nitrate and gives the test its name.

If the boiling tube is shaken very slightly, the aqueous layer will go uniformly brown (⑤).

In this test, care is taken not to mix the aqueous solution and the concentrated acid. If the contents of the tube were completely mixed, considerable heat would be generated and brown fumes of nitrogen dioxide would be evolved. The remaining liquid would be a yellow solution containing iron(III) ions.

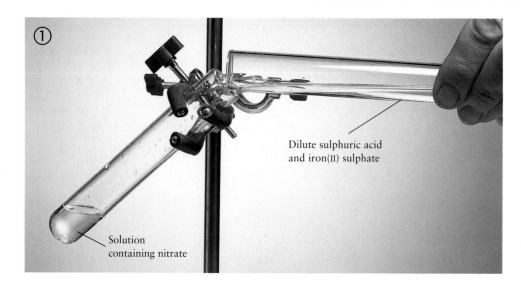

①

Dilute sulphuric acid and iron(II) sulphate

Solution containing nitrate

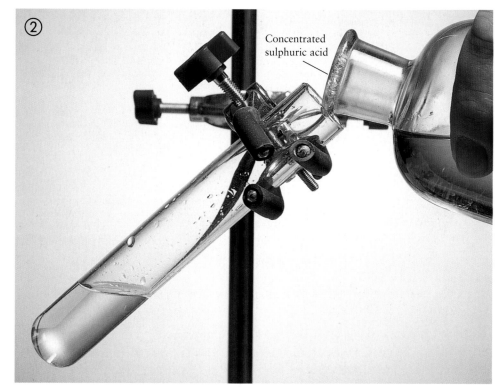

②

Concentrated sulphuric acid

A conspicuous brown ring

④

⑤

Testing for carbonate (CO_3^{2-}) ions

Carbonates are very common and include sodium carbonate, calcium carbonate (an important constituent of limestone) and magnesium carbonate.

Demonstration: test for carbonate by reaction with an acid

Carbonates, together with sulphides and nitrites (see the table on page 47), will evolve gas when reacted with an acid. In the case of a carbonate, it is carbon dioxide gas that is produced and tested for.

Dilute hydrochloric acid is added to the white powder suspected to contain a carbonate (①). The powder used in this demonstration is sodium carbonate.

The carbon dioxide produced can be tested for by bubbling it through limewater (②) which turns cloudy as particles of calcium carbonate are precipitated (③). Other tests for carbon dioxide are shown on page 24.

EQUATION: An acid and a carbonate produce carbon dioxide
Dilute hydrochloric acid + sodium carbonate ⇨ sodium chloride + carbon dioxide + water
$2HCl(aq) + Na_2CO_3(s) \Rightarrow 2NaCl(aq) + CO_2(g) + H_2O(l)$

IONIC EQUATION: Test for a carbonate
Aqueous hydrogen ions + carbonate ions ⇨ carbon dioxide + water
$2H^+(aq) + CO_3^{2-}(s) \Rightarrow CO_2(g) + H_2O(l)$

EQUATION: Carbon dioxide turns limewater cloudy
Carbon dioxide + calcium hydroxide ⇨ calcium carbonate + water
$CO_2(g) + Ca(OH)_2(aq) \Rightarrow CaCO_3(s) + H_2O(l)$

Testing for ammonium (NH$_4^+$) ions

The ammonium ion has a positive charge and so it is a cation. The presence of ammonium ions can be detected by warming the test solution with sodium hydroxide and then testing for ammonia being given off.

Demonstration: test for ammonium ions using sodium hydroxide

In this demonstration, sodium hydroxide solution is added to a boiling tube containing a sample of the solid compound which is suspected to contain ammonium ions (①) to make a solution (②).

If ammonium ions are present, they will react with the sodium hydroxide to release ammonia gas. However, ammonia gas is very soluble in cold water, so it may remain in the solution within the boiling tube. If this is the case, when wetted pH paper is placed in the mouth of the boiling tube, no alkaline gas – ammonia – is detected and the paper colour does not change (③ & ④).

To get over this possible difficulty, the solution is then warmed (⑤, see page 58). This makes the ammonia less soluble and ammonia gas is driven out of the solution and turns the pH paper blue (⑥, see page 58), indicating the presence of an alkaline gas. Ammonia is the only common alkaline gas (see page 34).

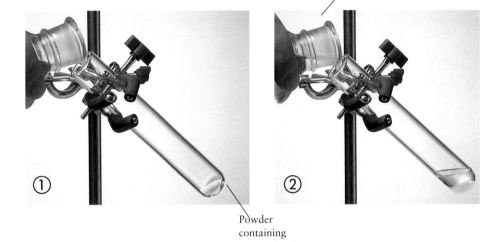

Sodium hydroxide solution is added.

① ②

Powder containing ammonium ions

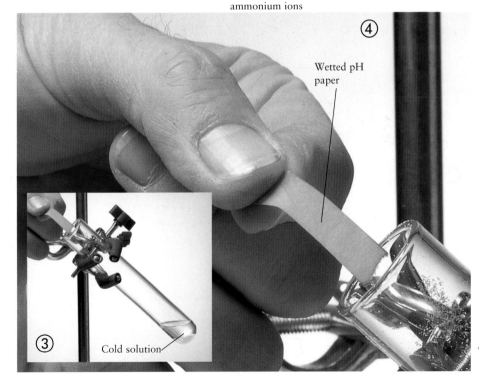

④

Wetted pH paper

③ Cold solution

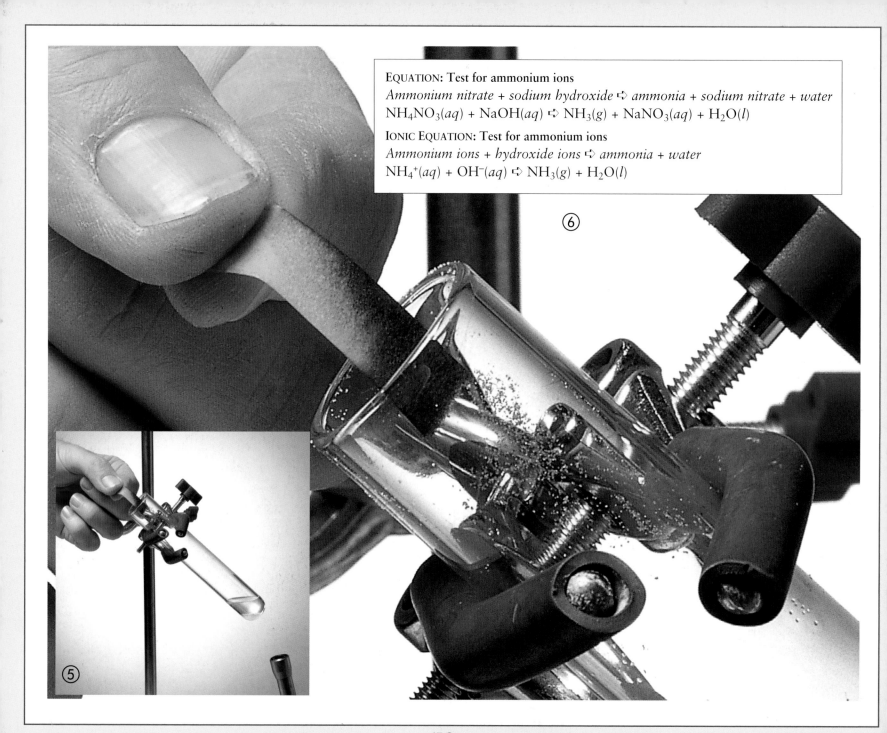

EQUATION: Test for ammonium ions
Ammonium nitrate + sodium hydroxide ⇨ ammonia + sodium nitrate + water
$NH_4NO_3(aq) + NaOH(aq) ⇨ NH_3(g) + NaNO_3(aq) + H_2O(l)$

IONIC EQUATION: Test for ammonium ions
Ammonium ions + hydroxide ions ⇨ ammonia + water
$NH_4^+(aq) + OH^-(aq) ⇨ NH_3(g) + H_2O(l)$

⑥

⑤

Testing for aluminium (Al^{3+}) ions

Aluminium ions are cations. As with most metals, testing involves producing an insoluble precipitate in a reaction with sodium hydroxide.

Demonstration: test for aluminium ions using sodium hydroxide

In this demonstration, colourless sodium hydroxide solution (①) in a pipette is added to aluminium sulphate in a test tube (②), and a colourless, gelatinous precipitate of aluminium hydroxide is formed (③).

If an excess of sodium hydroxide is added, this precipitate redissolves (④). However, it will not dissolve in excess ammonia solution.

EQUATION: Precipitation of aluminium hydroxide

Aluminium sulphate + sodium hydroxide ⇨ aluminium hydroxide + sodium sulphate

$$Al_2(SO_4)_3(aq) + 6NaOH(aq) \Rightarrow 2Al(OH)_3(s) + 3Na_2SO_4(aq)$$

IONIC EQUATION: Precipitation of aluminium hydroxide

Aluminium ions + hydroxide ions ⇨ aluminium hydroxide solid

$$Al^{3+}(aq) + 3OH^-(aq) \Rightarrow Al(OH)_3(s)$$

EQUATION: Redissolving aluminium hydroxide

Aluminium hydroxide solid + hydroxide ions ⇨ tetrahydroxoaluminate(III) ions

$$Al(OH)_3(s) + OH^-(aq) \Rightarrow Al(OH)_4^-(aq)$$

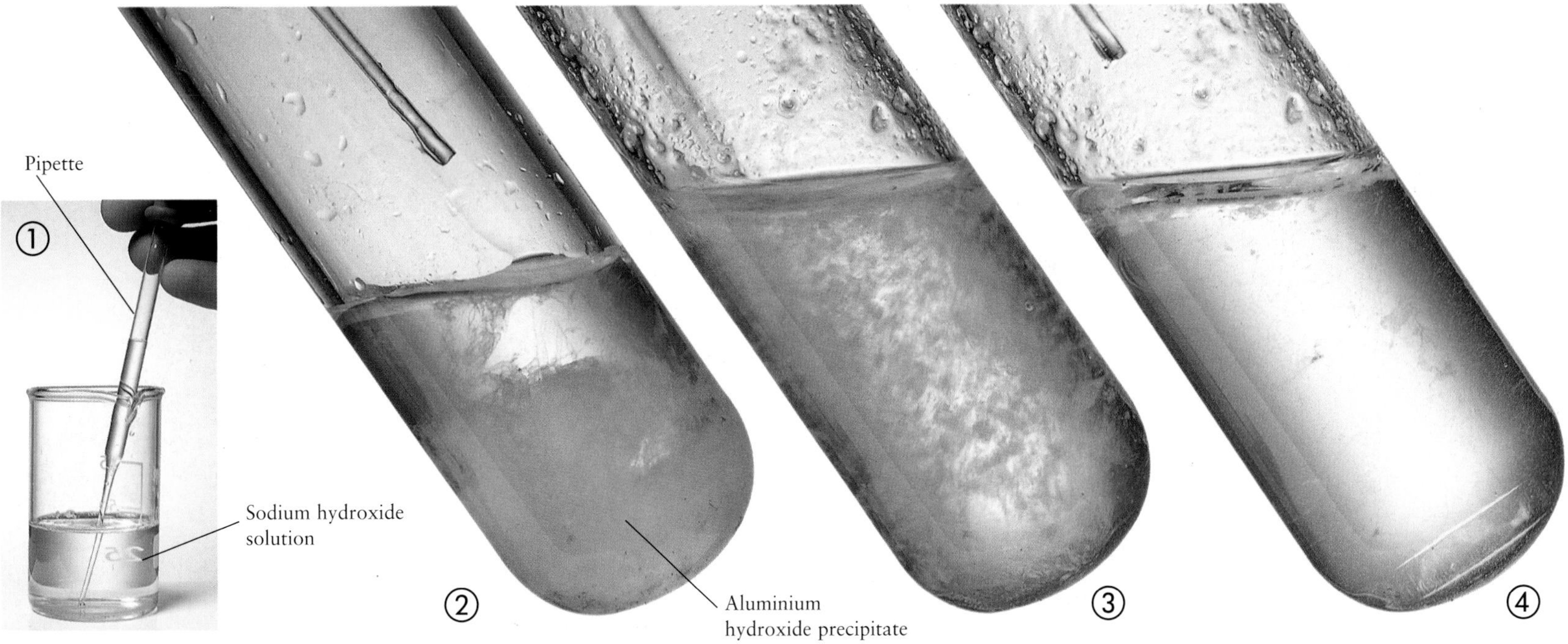

Pipette

① Sodium hydroxide solution

② Aluminium hydroxide precipitate

③

④

Testing for copper(II) (Cu^{2+}) ions

Copper(II) ions are cations, and compounds containing these ions usually have a characteristic blue colour.

Demonstration 1: test for copper(II) ions using sodium hydroxide

In this demonstration, colourless sodium hydroxide solution from a pipette is added to copper(II) sulphate solution in a boiling tube (①). A blue, gelatinous precipitate of copper(II) hydroxide forms (②).

    If more sodium hydroxide is added, no further change takes place. If ammonia solution is then added to the boiling tube, the gelatinous precipitate dissolves and a deep blue solution remains (see opposite page).

Demonstration 2: test for copper(II) ions using ammonia solution

In this demonstration, ammonia solution (ammonium hydroxide) from a pipette is added to some copper(II) sulphate solution in a boiling tube (③). A blue, gelatinous precipitate of copper(II) hydroxide forms (④). If an excess of ammonia solution is added, the copper(II) hydroxide precipitate redissolves and a deep blue solution of copper complex (Cu(NH$_3$)$_4^{2+}$(aq)) forms (⑤ & ⑥).

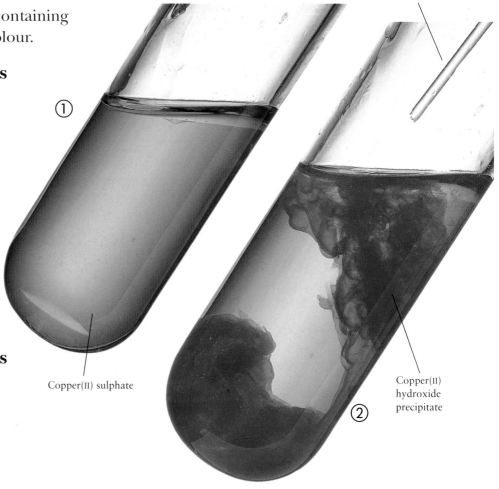

Sodium hydroxide solution is added from a pipette.

Copper(II) sulphate

Copper(II) hydroxide precipitate

EQUATION: Copper(II) sulphate and sodium hydroxide
Copper(II) sulphate + sodium hydroxide ⇨ copper(II) hydroxide + sodium sulphate
CuSO$_4$(aq) + 2NaOH(aq) ⇨ Cu(OH)$_2$(aq) + Na$_2$SO$_4$(aq)

IONIC EQUATION: Precipitation of copper(II) hydroxide
Copper ions + hydroxide ions ⇨ copper(II) hydroxide solid
Cu^{2+}(aq) + 2OH$^-$(aq) ⇨ Cu(OH)$_2$(s)

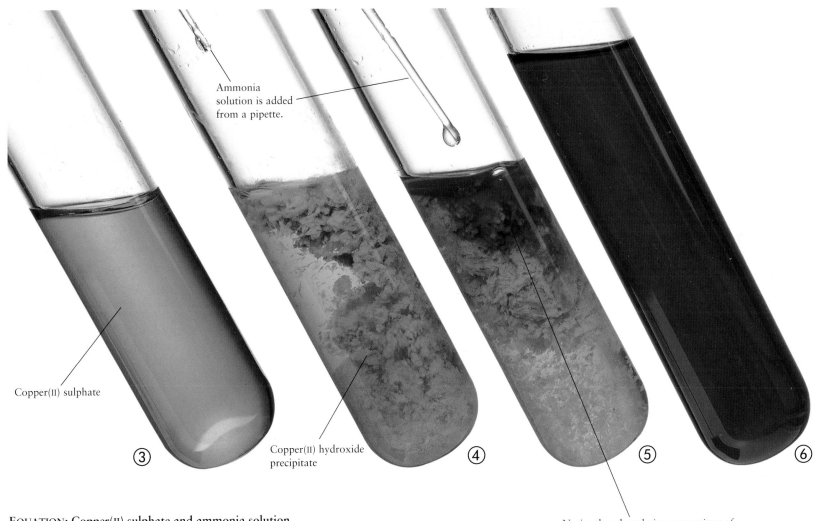

Ammonia solution is added from a pipette.

Copper(II) sulphate

Copper(II) hydroxide precipitate

③ ④ ⑤ ⑥

EQUATION: Copper(II) sulphate and ammonia solution

Copper(II) sulphate + ammonia solution ⇨ copper(II) hydroxide + ammonium sulphate

$CuSO_4(aq) + 2NH_4OH(aq) ⇨ Cu(OH)_2(aq) + (NH_4)_2SO_4(aq)$

EQUATION: Redissolving copper(II) hydroxide in excess ammonia solution

Copper(II) hydroxide solid + excess ammonia solution ⇨ copper ammine complex ions
+ hydroxide ions

$Cu(OH)_2(s) + 4NH_3(aq) ⇨ Cu(NH_3)_4^{2+}(aq) + 2OH^-(aq)$
Pale blue   Indigo blue

Notice that the relative proportions of reagents can make a difference to the products. In the lower part of the tube, the precipitate is pale blue because a relatively large amount of copper(II) sulphate has reacted with a relatively small amount of ammonia. At the top of the tube the opposite is true, and the solution is indigo blue. This is the copper ammine complex.

Testing for iron(II) (Fe^{2+}) ions

Iron(II) ions are cations whose compounds have a characteristic yellow–green colour.

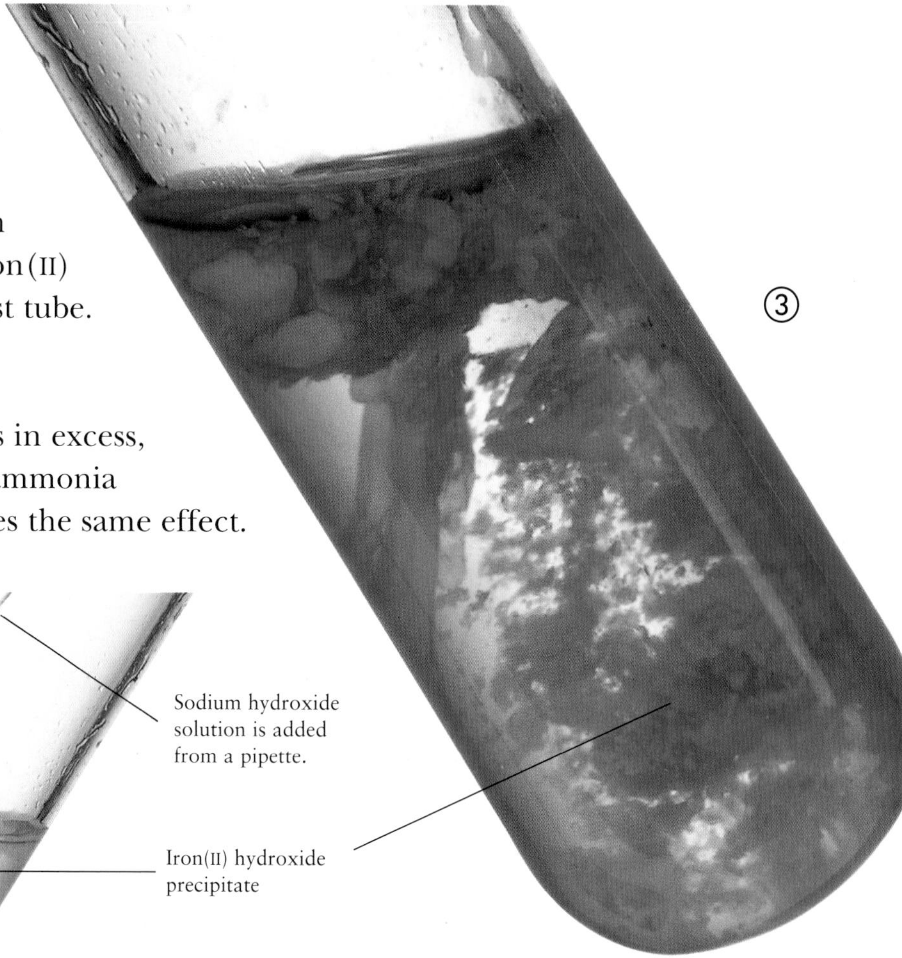

Demonstration: test for iron(II) ions using sodium hydroxide

In this demonstration, a small amount of sodium hydroxide solution from a pipette is added to iron(II) sulphate (ferrous sulphate) solution (①) in a test tube. A yellow–green gelatinous precipitate of iron(II) hydroxide (② & ③) forms.

If more sodium hydroxide is added until it is in excess, the precipitate still does not redissolve. Adding ammonia solution to a sample of iron(II) sulphate produces the same effect.

③

Iron(II) sulphate solution

Sodium hydroxide solution is added from a pipette.

Iron(II) hydroxide precipitate

①　②

EQUATION: Iron(II) chloride and sodium hydroxide
Iron(II) sulphate + sodium hydroxide ⇨ iron(II) hydroxide + sodium sulphate
$FeSO_4(aq) + 2NaOH(aq) \Rightarrow Fe(OH)_2(s) + 2Na_2SO_4(aq)$

IONIC EQUATION: Precipitation of iron(II) hydroxide
Iron(II) ions + hydroxide ions ⇨ iron(II) hydroxide solid
$Fe^{2+}(aq) + 2OH^-(aq) \Rightarrow Fe(OH)_2(s)$

Testing for iron(III) (Fe^{3+}) ions

Iron(III) ions are cations whose compounds are a characteristic rust red colour.

Demonstration: test for iron(III) ions using sodium hydroxide

In this demonstration, a small amount of sodium hydroxide solution from a pipette is added to iron(III) chloride (ferric chloride) solution in a test tube (①). It produces a reddish-brown gelatinous precipitate of iron(III) hydroxide (② & ③ detail).

Adding more sodium hydroxide to produce an excess has no effect.

Adding ammonia solution to a sample of iron(III) chloride produces the same effect.

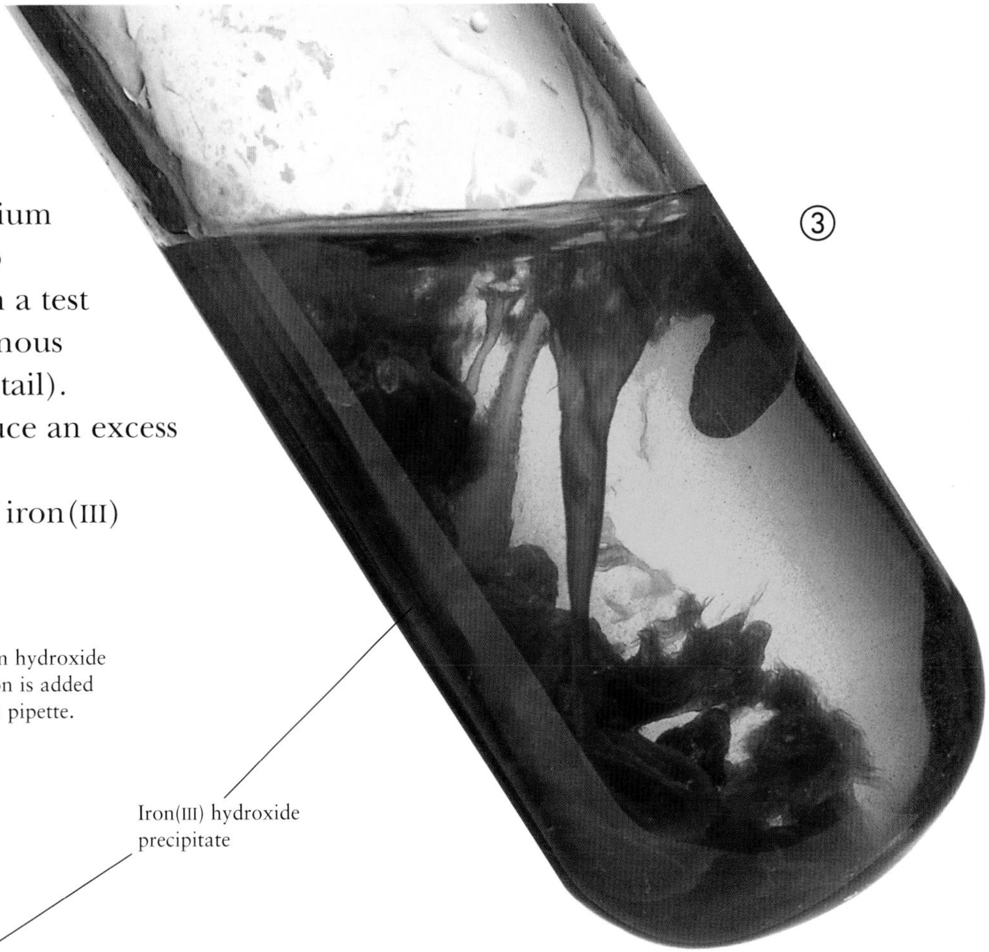

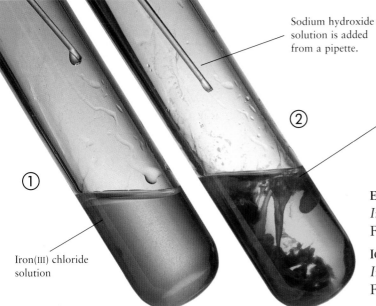

③

Sodium hydroxide solution is added from a pipette.

Iron(III) hydroxide precipitate

②

①

Iron(III) chloride solution

EQUATION: Iron(III) chloride and sodium hydroxide

Iron(III) chloride + sodium hydroxide ⇨ *iron(III) hydroxide + sodium chloride*

$FeCl_3(aq) + 3NaOH(aq)$ ⇨ $Fe(OH)_3(s) + 3NaCl(aq)$

IONIC EQUATION: Precipitation of iron(III) hydroxide

Iron(III) ions + hydroxide ions ⇨ *iron(III) hydroxide solid*

$Fe^{3+}(aq) + 3OH^-(aq)$ ⇨ $Fe(OH)_3(s)$

Testing for lead (Pb^{2+}) ions

Lead ions are cations. Tests produce a white precipitate, which must be carefully distinguished from other white precipitates.

Demonstration: test for lead ions using sodium hydroxide

When a small amount of sodium hydroxide solution is added to lead nitrate solution, a white precipitate of lead hydroxide forms (①). If more sodium hydroxide is added (②) until it is in excess, the lead hydroxide precipitate redissolves (③).

Alternatively, using ammonia solution (ammonium hydroxide) instead of sodium hydroxide also produces a white precipitate that will not redissolve in excess reagent.

Remarks

Note that this last test will distinguish between zinc (see page 65) and aluminium ions because aluminium hydroxide will not redissolve in excess ammonia solution.

Other distinguishing characteristics are that lead hydroxide is white and granular whereas the hydroxides of aluminium and zinc are white and have a gelatinous texture.

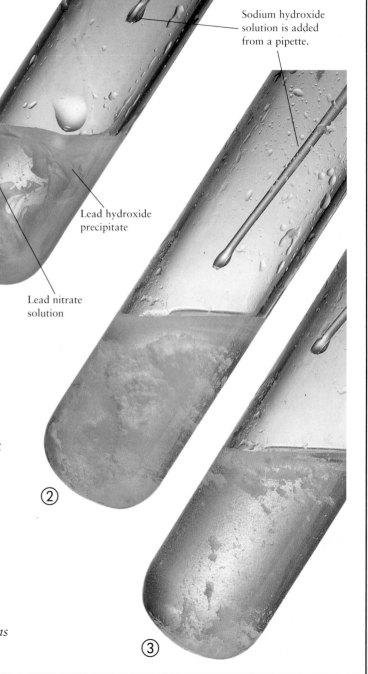

Sodium hydroxide solution is added from a pipette.

Lead hydroxide precipitate

Lead nitrate solution

①

②

③

EQUATION: Precipitation of lead hydroxide
Lead nitrate + sodium hydroxide ⇨ lead hydroxide + sodium nitrate
$Pb(NO_3)_2(aq) + 2NaOH(aq) \Rightarrow Pb(OH)_2(s) + 2NaNO_3(aq)$

IONIC EQUATION: Precipitation of lead hydroxide
Lead ions + hydroxide ions ⇨ lead hydroxide solid
$Pb^{2+}(aq) + 2OH^-(aq) \Rightarrow Pb(OH)_2(s)$

IONIC EQUATION: Redissolving lead hydroxide
Lead hydroxide solid + hydroxide ions ⇨ tetrahydroxoplumbate(II) ions
$Pb(OH)_2(s) + 2OH^-(aq) \Rightarrow Pb(OH)_4^{2-}(aq)$

Testing for zinc (Zn^{2+}) ions

Zinc ions are cations. Tests produce a white, gelatinous precipitate of zinc hydroxide that must be carefully distinguished from other white precipitates.

Demonstration: test for zinc ions using sodium hydroxide

When a small amount of sodium hydroxide solution from a pipette is added to a zinc compound (such as zinc sulphate solution) in a test tube (①), a white gelatinous precipitate of zinc hydroxide (②) forms. If more sodium hydroxide is added until it is in excess, the precipitate redissolves (③).

If ammonia solution is added to the zinc compound, this also produces a white precipitate of zinc hydroxide. If more ammonium hydroxide is added until it is in excess, the precipitate redissolves.

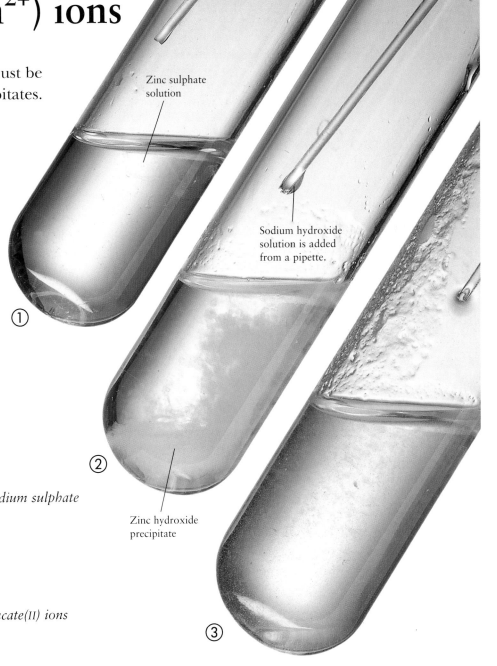

Zinc sulphate solution

Sodium hydroxide solution is added from a pipette.

① ② ③

Zinc hydroxide precipitate

EQUATION: Precipitation of zinc hydroxide
Zinc sulphate + sodium hydroxide ⇨ zinc hydroxide + sodium sulphate
$ZnSO_4(aq) + 2NaOH(aq) ⇨ Zn(OH)_2(s) + Na_2SO_4(aq)$

IONIC EQUATION: Precipitation of zinc hydroxide
Zinc ions + hydroxide ions ⇨ zinc hydroxide solid
$Zn^{2+}(aq) + 2OH^-(aq) ⇨ Zn(OH)_2(s)$

IONIC EQUATION: Redissolving zinc hydroxide
Zinc hydroxide solid + hydroxide ions ⇨ tetrahydroxozincate(II) ions
$Zn(OH)_2(s) + 2OH^-(aq) ⇨ Zn(OH)_4^{2-}(aq)$

MASTER GLOSSARY

absolute zero: the lowest possible temperature ($-273.15°C$).

absorption: the process by which a substance is soaked up. *See:* adsorption.

acid: a substance that can give a proton to another substance. Acids are compounds, containing hydrogen, that can attack and dissolve many substances. Acids are described as weak or strong, dilute or concentrated, mineral or organic. *Example:* hydrochloric acid (HCl). An acid in water can react with a base to form a salt and water.

acidic solution: a solution with a pH lower than 7.

acidity: a general term for the strength of an acid in a solution.

acid radical: the negative ion left behind when an acid loses a hydrogen ion. *Example:* Cl^- in hydrochloric acid (HCl).

acid salt: An ACID SALT contains at least one hydrogen ion and can behave as an acid in chemical reactions. Acid salts are produced under conditions that do not allow complete neutralisation of the acid. For example, sulphuric acid may react with a sodium compound to produce a normal sodium salt, sodium sulphate (Na_2SO_4), or it may retain some of the hydrogen, in which case it becomes the salt sodium hydrogen sulphate ($NaHSO_4$).

actinide series or actinide metals: a series of 15 similar radioactive elements between actinium and lawrencium. They are transition metals.

activated charcoal: a form of carbon, made up of tiny crystals of graphite, which is made by heating organic matter in the absence of air. It is then processed further to increase its pore space and therefore its surface area. Its surface area is about $2000\ m^2/g$. Activated charcoal readily adsorbs many gases and it is therefore widely used as a filter, for example, in gas masks.

activation energy: the energy required to make a reaction occur. The greater the activation energy of a reaction, the more its reaction rate depends on temperature. The activation energy of a reaction is useful because, if the rate of reaction is known at one temperature (for example, 100 °C) then the activation energy can be used to calculate the rate of reaction at another temperature (for example, 400 °C) without actually doing the experiment.

adsorption: the process by which a surface adsorbs a substance. The substances involved are not chemically combined and can be separated. *Example:* the adsorption properties of activated charcoal. *See:* absorption.

alchemy: the traditional 'art' of working with chemicals that prevailed through the Middle Ages. One of the main challenges for alchemists was to make gold from lead. Alchemy faded away as scientific chemistry was developed in the 17th century.

alcohol: an organic compound which contains a hydroxyl (OH) group. *Example:* ethanol (CH_3CH_2OH), also known as ethyl alcohol or grain alcohol.

alkali/alkaline: a base in (aqueous) solution. Alkalis react with, or neutralise, hydrogen ions in acids and have a pH greater than 7.0 because they contain relatively few hydrogen ions. *Example:* aqueous sodium hydroxide (NaOH).

alkaline cell (or battery): a dry cell in which the electrolyte contains sodium or potassium hydroxide.

alkaline earth metal: a member of Group 2 of the Periodic Table. *Example:* calcium.

alkali metals: a member of Group 1 of the Periodic Table. *Example:* sodium.

alkane: a hydrocarbon with no carbon-to-carbon multiple bonds. *Example:* ethane, C_2H_6.

alkene: a hydrocarbon with at least one carbon-to-carbon double bond. *Example:* ethene, C_2H_4.

alkyne: a hydrocarbon with at least one carbon-to-carbon triple bond. *Example:* ethyne, C_2H_2.

allotropes: alternative forms of an element that differ in the way the atoms are linked. *Example:* white and red phosphorus.

alloy: a mixture of a metal and various other elements. *Example:* brass is an alloy of copper and zinc.

amalgam: a liquid alloy of mercury with another metal.

amorphous: a solid in which the atoms are not arranged regularly (i.e. glassy). Compare crystalline.

amphoteric: a metal that will react with both acids and alkalis. *Example:* aluminium metal.

anhydrous: lacking water; water has been removed, for example, by heating. Many hydrated salts are crystalline. (Opposite of anhydrous is hydrous or hydrated.) *Example:* copper(II) sulphate can be anhydrous ($CuSO_4$) or hydrated ($CuSO_4 \bullet 5H_2O$).

anion: a negatively charged atom or group of atoms. *Examples:* chloride ion (Cl^-), hydroxide ion (OH^-).

anode: the electrode at which oxidation occurs; the negative terminal of a battery or the positive electrode of an electrolysis cell.

anodising: a process that uses the effect of electrolysis to make a surface corrosion resistant. *Example:* anodised aluminium.

antacid: a common name for any compound that reacts with stomach acid to neutralise it. *Example:* sodium hydrogen carbonate, also known as sodium bicarbonate.

antioxidant: a substance that reacts rapidly with radicals thereby preventing oxidation of some other substance.

anti-bumping granules: small glass or ceramic beads, designed to promote boiling without the development of large gas bubbles.

approximate relative atomic mass: *See:* relative atomic mass.

aqueous: a solution in which the solvent is water. Usually used as 'aqueous solution'. *Example:* aqueous solution of sodium hydroxide ($NaOH(aq)$).

aromatic hydrocarbons: compounds of carbon that have the benzene ring as part of their structure. *Examples:* benzene (C_6H_6), naphthalene ($C_{10}H_8$). They are known as aromatic because of the strong pungent smell given off by benzene.

atmospheric pressure: the pressure exerted by the gases in the air. Units of measurement are kilopascals (kPa), atmospheres (atm), millimetres of mercury (mm Hg) and Torr. Standard atmospheric pressure is 100 kPa, 1atm, 760 mm Hg or 760 Torr.

atom: the smallest particle of an element; a nucleus and its surrounding electrons.

atomic mass: the mass of an atom measured in atomic mass units (amu). An atomic mass unit is equal to one-twelfth of the atom of carbon-12. Atomic mass is now more generally used instead of atomic weight. *Example:* the atomic mass of chlorine is about 35 amu. *See:* atomic weight, relative atomic mass.

atomic number: also known as proton number. The number of electrons or the number of protons in an atom. *Example:* the atomic number of gold is 79 and for carbon it is 4.

atomic structure: the nucleus and the arrangement of electrons around the nucleus of an atom.

atomic weight: a common term used to mean the average molar mass of an element. This is the mass per mole of atoms. *Example:* the atomic weight of chlorine is about 35 g/mol. *See:* atomic mass, mole.

base: a substance that can accept a proton from another substance. *Example:* aqueous ammonia ($NH_3(aq)$). A base can react with an acid in water to form a salt and water.

basic salt: a salt that contains at least one hydroxide ion. The hydroxide ion can then behave as a base in chemical reactions. *Example:* the reaction of hydrochloric acid (HCl) with the base, aluminium hydroxide ($Al(OH)_3$) can form two basic salts, $Al(OH)_2Cl$ and $Al(OH)Cl_2$.

battery: a number of electrochemical cells placed in series.

bauxite: a hydrated impure oxide of aluminium ($Al_2O_3 \bullet xH_2O$, with the amount of water x being variable). It is the main ore used to obtain aluminium metal. The reddish-brown colour of bauxite is mainly caused by the iron oxide impurities it contains.

beehive shelf: an inverted earthenware bowl with a hole in the upper surface and a slot in the rim. Traditionally, the earthenware was brown and looked similar to a beehive, hence its name. A delivery tube passes through the slot and a gas jar is placed over the hole. This provides a convenient way to collect gas over water in a pneumatic trough.

bell jar: a tall glass jar with an open bottom and a wide, stoppered neck that is used in conjunction with a beehive shelf and a pneumatic trough in some experiments involving gases. The name derives from historic versions of the apparatus, which resembled a bell in shape.

blast furnace: a tall furnace charged with a mixture of iron ore, coke and limestone and used for the refining of iron metal. The name comes from the strong blast of air introduced during smelting.

bleach: a substance that removes colour in stains on materials, either by oxidising or reducing the staining compound. *Example:* sulphur dioxide (SO_2).

block: one of the main divisions of the Periodic Table. Blocks are named for the outermost, occupied electron shell of an element. *Example:* The Transition Metals all belong to the d-block.

boiling point: the temperature at which a liquid boils, changing from a liquid to a gas. Boiling points change with atmospheric pressure. *Example:* The boiling point of pure water at standard atmospheric pressure is 100 °C.

boiling tube: A thin glass tube closed at one end and used for chemical tests, etc. The composition and thickness of the glass is such that it cannot sustain very high temperatures and is intended for heating liquids to boiling point. *See:* side-arm boiling tube, test tube.

bond: chemical bonding is either a transfer or sharing of electrons by two or more atoms. There are a number of types of chemical bond, some very strong (such as covalent and ionic bonds), others weak (such as hydrogen bonds). Chemical bonds form because the linked molecule is more stable than the unlinked atoms from which it formed. *Example:* the hydrogen molecule (H_2) is more stable than single atoms of hydrogen, which is why hydrogen gas is always found as molecules of two hydrogen atoms.

Boyle's Law: At constant temperature, and for a given mass of gas, the volume of the gas (V) is inversely proportional to pressure that builds up (P): $P \propto 1/V$.

brine: a solution of salt (sodium chloride, NaCl) in water.

Büchner flask: a thick-walled side-arm flask designed to withstand the changes in pressure that occur when the flask is connected to a suction pump.

Büchner funnel: a special design of plastic or ceramic funnel which has a flat stage on which a filter paper can be placed. It is intended for use under suction with a Büchner funnel.

buffer (solution): a mixture of substances in solution that resists a change in the acidity or alkalinity of the solution when small amounts of an acid or alkali are added.

burette: a long, graduated glass tube with a tap at one end. A burette is used vertically, with the tap lowermost. Its main use is as a reservoir for a chemical during titration.

burn: a combustion reaction in which a flame is produced. A flame occurs where *gases* combust and release heat and light. At least two gases are therefore required if there is to be a flame. *Example:* methane gas (CH_4) burns in oxygen gas (O_2) to produce carbon dioxide (CO_2) and water (H_2O) and give out heat and light.

calorimeter: an insulated container designed to prevent heat gain or loss with the environment and thus allow changes of temperature within reacting chemicals to be measured accurately. It is named after the old unit of heat, the calorie.

capillary: a very small diameter (glass) tube. Capillary tubing has a small enough diameter to allow surface tension effects to retain water within the tube.

capillary action: the tendency for a liquid to be sucked into small spaces, such as between objects and through narrow-pore tubes. The force to do this comes from surface tension.

carbohydrate: a compound containing only carbon, hydrogen and oxygen. Carbohydrates have the formula $C_n(H_2O)_n$, where n is variable. *Example:* glucose ($C_6H_{12}O_6$).

carbonate: a salt of carbonic acid. Carbonate ions have the chemical formula CO_3^{2-}. *Examples:* calcium nitrate $CaCO_3$ and sodium carbonate Na_2CO_3.

catalyst: a substance that speeds up a chemical reaction, but itself remains unaltered at the end of the reaction. *Example:* copper in the reaction of hydrochloric acid with zinc.

catalytic converter: a device incorporated into some exhaust systems. The catalytic converter contains a framework and/or granules with a very large surface area and coated with catalysts that convert the pollutant gases passing over them into harmless products.

cathode: the electrode at which reduction occurs; the positive terminal of a battery or the negative electrode of an electrolysis cell.

cathodic protection: the technique of protecting a metal object by connecting it to a more readily oxidisable metal. The metal object being protected is made into the cathode of a cell. *Example:* iron can be protected by coupling it with magnesium. Iron forms the cathode and magnesium the anode.

cation: a positively charged ion. *Examples:* calcium ion (Ca^{2+}), ammonium ion (NH_4^+).

caustic: a substance that can cause burns if it touches the skin. *Example:* Sodium hydroxide, caustic soda (NaOH).

Celsius scale (°C): a temperature scale on which the freezing point of water is at 0 degrees and the normal boiling point at standard atmospheric pressure is 100 degrees.

cell: a vessel containing two electrodes and an electrolyte that can act as an electrical conductor.

centrifuge: an instrument for spinning small samples very rapidly. The fast spin causes the components of a mixture that have a different density to separate. This has the same effect as filtration.

ceramic: a material based on clay minerals which has been heated so that it has chemically hardened.

chalcogens: the members of Group 6 of the Periodic Table: oxygen, sulphur, selenium and tellurium. The word comes from the Greek meaning 'brass giver', because all these elements are found in copper ores, and copper is the most important metal in making brass.

change of state: a change between two of the three states of matter, solid, liquid and gas. *Example:* when water evaporates it changes from a liquid to a gaseous state.

Charles's Law: The volume (V) of a given mass of gas at constant pressure is directly proportional to its absolute temperature (T): $V \propto T$.

chromatography: A separation technique uses the ability of surfaces to adsorb substances with different strengths. The substances with the least adherence to the surface move faster and leave behind those that adhere more strongly.

coagulation: a term describing the tendency of small particles to stick together in clumps.

coherent: meaning that a substance holds together or sticks together well, and without holes or other defects. *Example:* Aluminium appears unreactive because, as soon as new metal is exposed to air, it forms a very complete oxide coating, which then stops further reaction occurring.

coinage metals: the elements copper, silver and gold, used to make coins.

coke: a solid substance left after the gases have been extracted from coal.

colloid: a mixture of ultramicroscopic particles dispersed uniformly through a second substance to form a suspension which may be almost like a solution or may set to a jelly (gel). The word comes from the Greek for glue.

colorimeter: an instrument for measuring the light-absorbing power of a substance. The absorption gives an accurate indication of the concentration of some coloured solutions.

combustion: a reaction in which an element or compound is oxidised to release energy. Some combustion reactions are slow, such as the combustion of the sugar we eat to provide our energy. If the combustion results in a flame, it is called burning. A flame occurs where *gases* combust and release heat and light. At least two gases are therefore required if there is to be a flame. *Example:* the combustion or burning of methane gas (CH_4) in oxygen gas (O_2) produces carbon dioxide (CO_2) and water (H_2O) and gives out heat and light. Some combustion reactions produce light and heat but do not produce flames. *Example:* the combustion of carbon in oxygen produces an intense red–white light but no flame.

combustion spoon: also known as a deflagrating spoon, it consists of a long metal handle with a small cup at the end. Its purpose is to allow the safe introduction of a (usually heated) substance into a gas jar filled with gas, when the reaction is likely to be vigorous. *Example:* the introduction of a heated sodium pellet into a gas jar containing chlorine.

compound: a chemical consisting of two or more elements chemically bonded together. *Example:* Calcium atoms can combine with carbon atoms and oxygen atoms to make calcium carbonate ($CaCO_3$), a compound of all three atoms.

condensation: the formation of a liquid from a gas. This is a change of state, also called a phase change.

condensation nuclei: microscopic particles of dust, salt and other materials suspended in the air, that attract water molecules. The usual result is the formation of water droplets.

condensation polymer: a polymer formed by a chain of reactions in which a water molecule is eliminated as every link of the

polymer is formed. *Examples:* polyesters, proteins, nylon.

conduction: (i) the exchange of heat (heat conduction) by contact with another object, or (ii) allowing the flow of electrons (electrical conduction).

conductivity: the ability of a substance to conduct. The conductivity of a solution depends on there being suitable free ions in the solution. A conducting solution is called an electrolyte. *Example:* dilute sulphuric acid.

convection: the exchange of heat energy with the surroundings produced by the flow of a fluid due to being heated or cooled.

corrosion: the oxidation of a metal. Corrosion is often regarded as unwanted and is more generally used to refer to the *slow* decay of a metal resulting from contact with gases and liquids in the environment. *Example:* Rust is the corrosion of iron.

corrosive: causing corrosion. *Example:* Sodium hydroxide (NaOH).

covalent bond: this is the most common form of strong chemical bonding and occurs when two atoms *share* electrons. *Example:* oxygen (O_2)

cracking: breaking down complex molecules into simpler compounds, as in oil refining.

crucible: a small bowl with a lip, made of heat-resistant white glazed ceramic. It is used for heating substances using a Bunsen flame.

crude oil: a chemical mixture of petroleum liquids. Crude oil forms the raw material for an oil refinery.

crystal: a substance that has grown freely so that it can develop external faces. Compare crystalline, where the atoms are not free to form individual crystals and amorphous, where the atoms are arranged irregularly.

crystalline: a solid in which the atoms, ions or molecules are organised into an orderly pattern without distinct crystal faces. *Examples:* copper(II) sulphate, sodium chloride. Compare amorphous.

crystallisation: the process in which a solute comes out of solution slowly and forms crystals. *See:* water of crystallisation.

crystal systems: seven patterns or systems into which all crystals can be grouped: cubic, hexagonal, rhombohedral, tetragonal, orthorhombic, monoclinic and triclinic.

cubic crystal system: groupings of crystals that look like cubes.

current: an electric current is produced by a flow of electrons through a conducting solid or ions through a conducting liquid. The rate of supply of this charge is measured in amperes (A).

decay (radioactive decay): the way that a radioactive element changes into another element due to loss of mass through radiation. *Example:* uranium 238 decays with the loss of an alpha particle to form thorium 234.

decomposition: the break down of a substance (for example, by heat or with the aid of a catalyst) into simpler components. In such a chemical reaction only one substance is involved. *Example:* hydrogen peroxide ($H_2O_2(aq)$) into oxygen ($O_2(g)$) and water ($H_2O(l)$).

decrepitation: when, as part of the decomposition of a substance, cracking sounds are also produced. *Example:* heating of lead nitrate ($Pb(NO_3)_2$).

dehydration: the removal of water from a substance by heating it, placing it in a dry atmosphere or using a drying (dehydrating) reagent such as concentrated sulphuric acid.

density: the mass per unit volume (e.g. g/cc).

desalinisation: the removal of all the salts from sea water, by reverse osmosis or heating the water and collecting the distillate. It is a very energy-intensive process.

desiccant: a substance that absorbs water vapour from the air. *Example:* silica gel.

desiccator: a glass bowl and lid containing a shelf. The apparatus is designed to store materials in dry air. A desiccant is placed below the shelf and the substance to be dried is placed on the shelf. The lid makes a gas-tight joint with the bowl.

destructive distillation: the heating of a material so that it decomposes entirely to release all of its volatile components. Destructive distillation is also known as pyrolysis.

detergent: a chemical based on petroleum that removes dirt.

Devarda's alloy: zinc with a trace of copper, which acts as a catalyst for reactions with the zinc.

diaphragm: a semipermeable membrane – a kind of ultrafine mesh filter – that allows only small ions to pass through. It is used in the electrolysis of brine.

diffusion: the slow mixing of one substance with another until the two substances are evenly mixed. Mixing occurs because of differences in concentration within the mixture. Diffusion works rapidly with gases, very slowly with liquids.

diffusion combustion: the form of combustion that occurs when two gases only begin to mix during ignition. As a result the flame is hollow and yellow in colour. *Example:* a candle flame.

dilute acid: an acid whose concentration has been reduced in a large proportion of water.

disinfectant: a chemical that kills bacteria and other microorganisms.

displacement reaction: a reaction that occurs because metals differ in their reactivity. If a more reactive metal is placed in a solution of a less reactive metal compound, a reaction occurs in which the more reactive metal displaces the metal ions in the solution. *Example:* when zinc metal is introduced into a solution of copper(II) sulphate (which thus contains copper ions), zinc goes into solution as zinc ions, while copper is displaced from the solution and forced to precipitate as metallic copper.

dissociate: to break bonds apart. In the case of acids, it means to break up, forming hydrogen ions. This is an example of ionisation. Strong acids dissociate completely. Weak acids are not completely ionised, and a solution of a weak acid has a relatively low concentration of hydrogen ions.

dissolve: to break down a substance in a solution without causing a reaction.

distillation: the process of separating mixtures by condensing the vapours through cooling.

distilled water: distilled water is nearly pure water and is produced by distillation of tap water. Distilled water is used in the laboratory in preference to tap water because the distillation process removes many of the impurities in tap water that may influence the chemical reactions for which the water is used.

Dreschel bottle: a tall bottle with a special stopper, designed to allow a gas to pass through a liquid. The stopper contains both inlet and outlet tubes. One tube extends below the surface of the liquid so that the gas has to pass through the liquid before it can escape to the outlet tube.

dropper funnel: a special funnel with a tap to allow the controlled release of a liquid. Also known as a dropping funnel or tap funnel.

drying agent: *See:* dehydrating agent.

dye: a coloured substance that will stick to another substance so that both appear coloured.

effervesce: to give off bubbles of gas.

effloresce: to lose water and turn to a fine powder on exposure to the air. *Example:* Sodium carbonate on the rim of a reagent bottle stopper.

electrical conductivity: *See:* conductivity

electrical potential: the energy produced by an electrochemical cell and measured by the voltage or electromotive force (emf). *See:* potential difference, electromotive force.

electrochemical cell: a cell consisting of two electrodes and an electrolyte. It can be set up to generate an electric current (usually known as a galvanic cell, an example of which is a battery), or an electric current can be passed through it to produce a chemical reaction (in which case it is called an electrolytic cell and can be used to refine metals or for electroplating).

electrochemical series: the arrangement of substances that are either oxidising or reducing agents in order of strength as a reagent, for example, with the strong oxidising agents at the top of the list and the strong reducing agents at the bottom.

electrode: a conductor that forms one terminal of a cell.

electrolysis: an electrical–chemical process that uses an electric current to cause the break-up of a compound and the movement of metal ions in a solution. The process happens in many natural situations (as for example in rusting) and is also commonly used

in industry for purifying (refining) metals or for plating metal objects with a fine, even metal coating.

electrolyte: an ionic solution that conducts electricity.

electrolytic cell: *See:* electrochemical cell.

electromotive force (emf): the force set up in an electric circuit by a potential difference.

electron: a tiny, negatively charged particle that is part of an atom. The flow of electrons through a solid material such as a wire produces an electric current.

electron configuration: the pattern in which electrons are arranged in shells around the nucleus of an atom. *Example:* chlorine has the configuration 2, 8, 7.

electroplating: depositing a thin layer of a metal on to the surface of another substance using electrolysis.

element: a substance that cannot be decomposed into simpler substance by chemical means. *Examples:* calcium, iron, gold.

emulsion: tiny droplets of one substance dispersed in another. One common oil in water emulsion is called milk. Because the tiny droplets tend to come together, another stabilising substance is often needed. Soaps and detergents are such agents, wrapping the particles of grease and oil in a stable coat. Photographic film is an example of a solid emulsion.

endothermic reaction: a reaction that takes in heat. *Example:* when ammonium chloride is dissolved in water.

end point: the stage in a titration when the reaction between the titrant (added from a burette) and the titrate (in the flask) is complete. The end point is normally recognised by use of an indicator which has been added to

the titrate. In an acid–base reaction this is also called the neutralisation point.

enzyme: biological catalysts in the form of proteins in the body that speed up chemical reactions. Every living cell contains hundreds of enzymes that help the processes of life continue.

ester: organic compounds formed by the reaction of an alcohol with an acid and which often have a fruity taste. *Example:* ethyl acetate ($CH_3COOC_2H_5$).

evaporation: the change of state of a liquid to a gas. Evaporation happens below the boiling point and is used as a method of separating the materials in a solution.

excess, to: if a reactant has been added to another reactant in excess, it has exceeded the amount required to complete the reaction.

exothermic reaction: a reaction that gives out substantial amounts of heat. *Example:* sucrose and concentrated sulphuric acid.

explosive: a substance which, when a shock is applied to it, decomposes very rapidly, releasing a very large amount of heat and creating a large volume of gases as a shock wave.

fats: semisolid, energy-rich compounds derived from plants or animals, made of carbon, hydrogen and oxygen. These are examples of esters.

ferment: to break down a substance by microorganisms in the absence of oxygen. *Example:* fermentation of sugar to ethanol during the production of alcoholic drinks.

filtrate: the liquid that has passed through a filter.

filtration: the separation of a liquid from a solid using a membrane with small holes (i.e. a filter paper).

flame: a mixture of gases undergoing burning. A solid or liquid must produce a gas before it can react with oxygen and burn with a flame.

flammable (also inflammable): able to burn (in air). *Opposite:* non-flammable.

flocculation: the grouping together of small particles in a suspension to form particles large enough to settle out as a precipitate. Flocculation is usually caused by the presence of a flocculating agent. *Example:* calcium ions are the flocculating agent for suspended clay particles.

fluid: able to flow; either a liquid or a gas.

fluorescent: a substance that gives out visible light when struck by invisible waves, such as ultraviolet rays.

flux: a material used to make it easier for a liquid to flow. A flux dissolves metal oxides and so prevents a metal from oxidising while being heated.

foam: a substance that is sufficiently gelatinous to be able to contain bubbles of gas. The gas bulks up the substance, making it behave as though it were semirigid.

fossil fuels: hydrocarbon compounds that have been formed from buried plant and animal remains. High pressures and temperatures lasting over millions of years are required. *Examples:* The fossil fuels are coal, oil and natural gas.

fraction: a group of similar components of a mixture. *Example:* In the petroleum industry the light fractions of crude oil are those with the smallest molecules, while the medium and heavy fractions have larger molecules.

fractional distillation: the separation of the components of a liquid mixture by heating them to their boiling points.

fractionating column: a glass column designed to allow different fractions to be separated when they boil. In industry, it may be called a fractionating tower.

free radical: a very reactive atom or group with a 'spare' electron. *Example:* methyl, $CH_3\bullet$.

freezing point: the temperature at which a substance undergoes a phase change from a liquid to a solid. It is the same temperature as the melting point.

fuel: a concentrated form of chemical energy. The main sources of fuels (called fossil fuels because they were formed by geological processes) are coal, crude oil and natural gas.

fuel rods: the rods of uranium or other radioactive material used as a fuel in nuclear power stations.

fume chamber or fume cupboard: a special laboratory chamber fitted with a protective glass shield and containing a powerful extraction fan to remove toxic fumes.

fuming: an unstable liquid that gives off a gas. Very concentrated acid solutions are often fuming solutions. *Example:* fuming nitric acid.

galvanising: applying a thin zinc coating to protect another metal.

gamma rays: waves of radiation produced as the nucleus of a radioactive element rearranges itself into a tighter cluster of protons and neutrons. Gamma rays carry enough energy to damage living cells.

gangue: the unwanted material in an ore.

gas/gaseous phase: a form of matter in which the molecules form no definite shape and are free to move about to uniformly fill any vessel they are put in. A gas can easily be compressed into a much smaller volume.

gas syringe: a glass syringe with a graduated cylinder designed to collect and measure small amounts of gases produced during an experiment.

gelatinous precipitate: a precipitate that has a jelly-like appearance. *Example*: iron (III) hydroxide. Because a gelatinous precipitate is mostly water, it is of a similar density to water and will float or lie suspended in the liquid. *See*: granular precipitate.

glass: a transparent silicate without any crystal growth. It has a glassy lustre and breaks with a curved fracture. Note that some minerals have all these features and are therefore natural glasses. Household glass is a synthetic silicate.

glucose: the most common of the natural sugars ($C_6H_{12}O_6$). It occurs as the polymer known as cellulose, the fibre in plants. Starch is also a form of glucose.

granular precipitate: a precipitate that has a grain-like appearance. *Example*: lead(II) hydroxide. *See*: gelatinous precipitate.

gravimetric analysis: a quantitative form of analysis in which the mass (weight) of the reactants and products is measured.

group: a vertical column in the Periodic Table. There are eight groups in the table. Their numbers correspond to the number of electrons in the outer shell of the atoms in the group. *Example*: Group 1: member, sodium.

Greenhouse Effect: an increase in the global air temperature as a result of heat released from burning fossil fuels being absorbed by carbon dioxide in the atmosphere.

Greenhouse gas: any of various the gases that contribute to the Greenhouse Effect. *Example*: carbon dioxide.

half-life: the time it takes for the radiation coming from a sample of a radioactive element to decrease by half.

halide: a salt of one of the halogens.

halogen: one of a group of elements including chlorine, bromine, iodine and fluorine in Group 7 of the Periodic Table.

heat: the energy that is transferred when a substance is at a different temperature to that of its surroundings. *See*: endothermic and exothermic reactions.

heat capacity: the ratio of the heat supplied to a substance, compared with the rise in temperature that is produced.

heat of combustion: the amount of heat given off by a mole of a substance during combustion. This heat is a property of the substance and is the same no matter what kind of combustion is involved. *Example*: heat of combustion of carbon is 94.05 kcal (x 4.18 = 393.1 kJ).

hydrate: a solid compound in crystalline form that contains water molecules. Hydrates commonly form when a solution of a soluble salt is evaporated. The water that forms part of a hydrate crystal is known as the 'water of crystallisation'. It can usually be removed by heating, leaving an anhydrous salt.

hydration: the process of absorption of water by a substance. In some cases hydration makes the substance change colour; in many other cases there is no colour change, simply a change in volume. *Example*: dark blue hydrated copper(II) sulphate ($CuSO_4 \bullet 5H_2O$) can be heated to produce white anhydrous copper(II) sulphate ($CuSO_4$).

hydride: a compound containing just hydrogen and another element, most often a metal.

Examples: water (H_2O), methane (CH_4) and phosphine (PH_3).

hydrous: hydrated with water. *See*: anhydrous.

hydrocarbon: a compound in which only hydrogen and carbon atoms are present. Most fuels are hydrocarbons, as is the simple plastic, polyethene. *Example*: methane CH_4.

hydrogen bond: a type of attractive force that holds one molecule to another. It is one of the weaker forms of intermolecular attractive force. *Example*: hydrogen bonds occur in water.

ignition temperature: the temperature at which a substance begins to burn.

immiscible: will not mix with another substance. e.g., oil and water.

incandescent: glowing or shining with heat. *Example*: tungsten filament in an incandescent light bulb.

incomplete combustion: combustion in which only some of the reactant or reactants combust, or the products are not those that would be obtained if all the reactions went to completion. It is uncommon for combustion to be complete and incomplete combustion is more frequent. *Example*: incomplete combustion of carbon in oxygen produces carbon monoxide and not carbon dioxide.

indicator (acid–base indicator): a substance or mixture of substances used to test the acidity or alkalinity of a substance. An indicator changes colour depending on the acidity of the solution being tested. Many indicators are complicated organic substances. Some indicators used in the laboratory include Universal Indicator, litmus, phenolphthalein, methyl orange and bromothymol. *See*: Universal Indicator.

induction period: the time taken for a reaction to reach ignition temperature. During this period, no apparent reaction occurs, then the materials appear to undergo spontaneous combustion.

inert: unreactive.

inhibitor: a substance that prevents a reaction from occurring.

inorganic substance: a substance that does not contain carbon and hydrogen. *Examples*: NaCl, $CaCO_3$.

insoluble: a substance that will not dissolve.

ion: an atom, or group of atoms, that has gained or lost one or more electrons and so developed an electrical charge. Ions behave differently from electrically neutral atoms and molecules. They can move in an electric field, and they can also bind strongly to solvent molecules such as water. Positively charged ions are called cations; negatively charged ions are called anions. Ions can carry an electrical current through solutions.

ionic bond: the form of bonding that occurs between two ions when the ions have opposite charges. *Example*: sodium cations bond with chloride anions to form common salt (NaCl) when a salty solution is evaporated. Ionic bonds are strong bonds except in the presence of a solvent. *See*: bond.

ionic compound: a compound that consists of ions. *Example*: NaCl.

ionise: to break up neutral molecules into oppositely charged ions or to convert atoms into ions by the loss of electrons.

ionisation: a process that creates ions.

isotope: an atom that has the same number of protons in its nucleus, but which has a different mass. *Example*: carbon 12 and carbon 14.

Kipp's apparatus: a piece of glassware consisting of three

chambers, designed to provide a continuous and regulated production of gas by bringing the reactants into contact in a controlled way.

lanthanide series or lanthanide metals: a series of 15 similar metallic elements between lanthanum and lutetium. They are transition metals and also also called rare earths.

latent heat: the amount of heat that is absorbed or released during the process of changing state between gas, liquid or solid. For example, heat is absorbed when a substance melts and it is released again when the substance solidifies.

lattice: a regular arrangement of atoms, ions or molecules in a crystalline solid.

leaching: the extraction of a substance by percolating a solvent through a material. *Example*: when water flows through an ore, some of the heavy metals in it may be leached out causing environmental pollution.

Liebig condenser: a piece of glassware consisting of a sloping water-cooled tube. The design allows a volatile material to be condensed and collected.

liquefaction: to make something liquid.

liquid/liquid phase: a form of matter that has a fixed volume but no fixed shape.

lime (quicklime): calcium oxide (CaO). A white, caustic solid, manufactured by heating limestone and used for making mortar, fertiliser or bleach.

limewater: an aqueous solution of calcium hydroxide, used especially to detect the presence of carbon dioxide.

litmus: an indicator obtained from lichens. Used as a solution or impregnated into paper (litmus paper), which is dampened before use. Litmus turns red under acid conditions and purple in alkaline conditions. Litmus is a crude indicator when compared with Universal Indicator.

load (electronics): an impedance or circuit that receives or develops the output of a cell or other power supply.

lustre: the shininess of a substance.

malleable: able to be pressed or hammered into shape.

manometer: a device for measuring gas pressure. A simple manometer is made by partly filling a U-shaped rubber tube with water and connecting one end to the source of gas whose pressure is to be measured. The pressure is always relative to atmospheric pressure.

mass: the amount of matter in an object. In everyday use the word weight is often used (somewhat incorrectly) to mean mass.

matter: anything that has mass and takes up space.

melting point: the temperature at which a substance changes state from a solid phase to a liquid phase. It is the same as freezing point.

membrane: a thin, flexible sheet. A semipermeable membrane has microscopic holes of a size that will selectively allow some ions and molecules to pass through but hold others back. It thus acts as a kind of filter. *Example:* a membrane used for osmosis.

meniscus: the curved surface of a liquid that forms in a small bore or capillary tube. The meniscus is convex (bulges upwards) for mercury and is concave (sags downwards) for water.

metal: a class of elements that is a good conductor of electricity and heat, has a metallic lustre, is malleable and ductile, forms cations and has oxides that are bases. Metals are formed as cations

held together by a sea of electrons. A metal may also be an alloy of these elements. *Example:* sodium, calcium, gold. *See:* alloy, metalloid, non-metal.

metallic bonding: cations reside in a 'sea' of mobile electrons. It allows metals to be good conductors and means that they are not brittle. *See:* bonding.

metallic lustre: *See:* lustre.

metalloid: a class of elements intermediate in properties between metals and non-metals. Metalloids are also called semi-metals or semiconductors. *Example:* silicon, germanium, antimony. *See:* metal, non-metal, semiconductor.

micronutrient: an element that the body requires in small amounts. Another term is trace element.

mineral: a solid substance made of just one element or compound. *Example:* calcite is a mineral because it consists only of calcium carbonate; halite is a mineral because it contains only sodium chloride.

mineral acid: an acid that does not contain carbon and which attacks minerals. Hydrochloric, sulphuric and nitric acids are the main mineral acids.

miscible: capable of being mixed.

mixing combustion: the form of combustion that occurs when two gases thoroughly mix before they ignite and so produce almost complete combustion. *Example:* when a Bunsen flame is blue.

mixture: a material that can be separated into two or more substances using physical means. *Example:* a mixture of copper(II) sulphate and cadmium sulphide can be separated by filtration.

molar mass: the mass per mole of atoms of an element. It has the same value and uses the same units as atomic weight. *Example:* molar mass of chlorine is 35.45 g/mol. *See:* atomic weight.

mole: 1 mole is the amount of a substance which contains Avagadro's number (6×10^{23}) of particles. *Example:* 1 mole of carbon-12 weighs exactly 12 g.

molecular mass: *See:* molar mass.

molecular weight: *See:* molar mass.

molecule: a group of two or more atoms held together by chemical bonds. *Example:* O_2.

monoclinic system: a grouping of crystals that look like double-ended chisel blades.

monomer: a small molecule and building block for larger chain molecules or polymers ('mono' means one, 'mer' means part). *Examples:* tetrafluoroethene for teflon, ethene for polyethene.

native element: an element that occurs in an uncombined state. *Examples:* sulphur, gold.

native metal: a pure form of a metal, not combined as a compound. Native metal is more common in poorly reactive elements than in those that are very reactive. *Examples:* copper, gold.

net ionic reaction: the overall, or net, change that occurs in a reaction, seen in terms of ions.

neutralisation: the reaction of acids and bases to produce a salt and water. The reaction causes hydrogen from the acid and hydroxide from the base to be changed to water. *Example:* hydrochloric acid reacts with, and neutralises, sodium hydroxide to form the salt sodium chloride (common salt) and water. The term is more generally used for any reaction in which the pH changes toward 7.0, which is the pH of a neutral solution. *See:* pH.

neutralisation point: *See:* end point.

neutron: a particle inside the nucleus of an atom that is neutral and has no charge.

newton (N): the unit of force required to give one kilogram an acceleration of one metre per second every second (1 ms^{-2}).

nitrate: a compound that includes nitrogen and oxygen and contains more oxygen than a nitrite. Nitrate ions have the chemical formula NO_3^-. *Examples:* sodium nitrate $NaNO_3$ and lead nitrate $Pb(NO_3)_2$.

nitrite: a compound that includes nitrogen and oxygen and contains less oxygen than a nitrate. Nitrite ions have the chemical formula NO_2^-. *Example:* sodium nitrite $NaNO_2$.

noble gases: the members of Group 8 of the Periodic Table: helium, neon, argon, krypton, xenon, radon. These gases are almost entirely unreactive.

noble metals: silver, gold, platinum and mercury. These are the least reactive metals.

non-combustible: a substance that will not combust or burn. *Example:* carbon dioxide.

non-metal: a brittle substance that does not conduct electricity. *Examples:* sulphur, phosphorus, all gases. *See:* metal, metalloid.

normal salt: salts that do not contain a hydroxide (OH$^-$) ion, which would make them basic salts, or a hydrogen ion, which would make them acid salts. *Example:* sodium chloride (NaCl).

nucleus: the small, positively charged particle at the centre of an atom. The nucleus is responsible for most of the mass of an atom.

opaque: a substance that will not transmit light so that it is impossible to see through it. Most solids are opaque.

ore: a rock containing enough of a useful substance to make mining it worthwhile. *Example:* bauxite, aluminium ore.

organic acid: an acid containing carbon and hydrogen. *Example:* methanoic (formic) acid (HCOOH).

organic chemistry: the study of organic compounds.

organic compound (organic substance; organic material): a compound (or substance) that contains carbon and usually hydrogen. (The carbonates are usually excluded.) *Examples:* methane (CH_4), chloromethane (CH_3Cl), ethene (C_2H_4), ethanol (C_2H_5OH), ethanoic acid (C_2H_3OOH), etc.

organic solvent: an organic substance that will dissolve other substances. *Example:* carbon tetrachloride (CCl_4).

osmosis: a process whereby molecules of a liquid solvent move through a semipermeable membrane from a region of low concentration of a solute to a region with a high concentration of a solute.

oxidation–reduction reaction (redox reaction): reaction in which oxidation and reduction occurs; a reaction in which electrons are transferred. *Example:* copper and oxygen react to produce copper(II) oxide. The copper is oxidised, and oxygen is reduced.

oxidation: combination with oxygen or a reaction in which an atom, ion or molecule loses electrons to an oxidising agent. (Note that an oxidising agent does not have to contain oxygen.) The opposite of oxidation is reduction. *See:* reduction.

oxidation number (oxidation state): the effective charge on an atom in a compound. An increase in oxidation number corresponds to oxidation, and a decrease to reduction. Shown in Roman numerals. *Example:* manganate(IV).

oxidation state: *See:* oxidation number.

oxide: a compound that includes oxygen and one other element. *Example:* copper oxide (CuO).

oxidise: to combine with or gain oxygen or to react such that an atom, ion or molecule loses electrons to an oxidising agent.

oxidising agent: a substance that removes electrons from another substance being oxidised (and therefore is itself reduced) in a redox reaction. *Example:* chlorine (Cl_2).

ozone: a form of oxygen whose molecules contain three atoms of oxygen. Ozone is regarded as a beneficial gas when high in the atmosphere because it blocks ultraviolet rays. It is a harmful gas when breathed in, so low level ozone which is produced as part of city smog is regarded as a form of pollution. The ozone layer is the uppermost part of the stratosphere.

partial pressure: the pressure a gas in a mixture would exert if it alone occupied a flask. *Example:* oxygen makes up about a fifth of the atmosphere. Its partial pressure is therefore about a fifth of normal atmospheric pressure.

pascal: the unit of pressure, equal to one newton per square metre of surface. *See:* newton.

patina: a surface coating that develops on metals and protects them from further corrosion. *Example:* the green coating of copper carbonate that forms on copper statues.

percolate: to move slowly through the pores of a rock.

period: a row in the Periodic Table.

Periodic Table: a chart organising elements by atomic number and chemical properties into groups and periods.

pestle and mortar: a pestle is a ceramic rod with a rounded end, a mortar is a ceramic dish. Pestle and mortar are used together to pound or grind solids into fine powders.

Petri dish: a shallow glass or plastic dish with a lid.

petroleum: a natural mixture of a range of gases, liquids and solids derived from the decomposed remains of plants and animals.

pH: a measure of the hydrogen ion concentration in a liquid. Neutral is pH 7.0; numbers greater than this are alkaline; smaller numbers are acidic. *See:* neutralisation, acid, base.

pH meter: a device that accurately measures the pH of a solution. A pH meter is a voltmeter that measures the electric potential difference between two electrodes (which are attached to the meter through a probe) when they are submerged in a solution. The readings are shown on a dial or digital display.

phase: a particular state of matter. A substance may exist as a solid, liquid or gas and may change between these phases with addition or removal of energy. *Examples:* ice, liquid and vapour are the three phases of water. Ice undergoes a phase change to water when heat energy is added.

phosphor: any material that glows when energised by ultraviolet or electron beams, such as in fluorescent tubes and cathode ray tubes. Phosphors, such as phosphorus, emit light after the source of excitation is cut off. This is why they glow in the dark. By contrast, fluorescers, such as fluorite, only emit light while they are being excited by ultraviolet light or an electron beam.

photochemical smog: photochemical reactions are caused by the energy of sunlight. Photochemical smog is a mixture of tiny particles and a brown haze caused by the reaction of colourless nitric oxide from vehicle exhausts and oxygen of the air to form brown nitrogen dioxide.

photon: a parcel of light energy.

photosynthesis: the process by which plants use the energy of the Sun to make the compounds they need for life. In photosynthesis, six molecules of carbon dioxide from the air combine with six molecules of water, forming one molecule of glucose (sugar) and releasing six molecules of oxygen back into the atmosphere.

pipe-clay triangle: a device made from three small pieces of ceramic tube which are wired together in the shape of a triangle. Pipe-clay triangles are used to support round-bottomed dishes when they are heated in a Bunsen flame.

pipette: a log, slender, glass tube used, in conjunction with a pipette filler, to draw up and then transfer accurately measured amounts of liquid.

plastic: (material) a carbon-based substance consisting of long chains (polymers) of simple molecules. The word plastic is commonly restricted to synthetic polymers. *Examples:* polyvinyl chloride, nylon: **(property)** a material is plastic if it can be made to change shape easily. Plastic materials will remain in the new shape. (Compare with elastic, a property whereby a material goes back to its original shape.)

pneumatic trough: a shallow water-filled glass dish used to house a beehive shelf and a gas jar as part of the apparatus for collecting a gas over water.

polar solvent: a solvent in which the atoms have partial electric charges. *Example:* water.

polymer: a compound that is made of long chains by combining molecules (called monomers) as repeating units. ('Poly' means many, 'mer' means part.) *Examples:* polytetrafluoroethene or Teflon from tetrafluoroethene, Terylene from terephthalic acid and ethane-1,2-diol (ethylene glycol).

polymerisation: a chemical reaction in which large numbers of similar molecules arrange themselves into large molecules, usually long chains. This process usually happens when there is a suitable catalyst present. *Example:* ethene gas reacts to form polyethene in the presence of certain catalysts.

polymorphism: (meaning many shapes) the tendency of some materials to have more than one solid form. *Example:* carbon as diamond, graphite and buckminsterfullerene.

porous: a material containing many small holes or cracks. Quite often the pores are connected, and liquids, such as water or oil, can move through them.

potential difference: a measure of the work that must be done to move an electric charge from one point to the other in a circuit. Potential difference is measured in volts, V. *See:* electrical potential.

precious metal: silver, gold, platinum, iridium and palladium. Each is prized for its rarity.

precipitate: a solid substance formed as a result of a chemical reaction between two liquids or gases. *Example:* iron(III) hydroxide is precipitated when sodium hydroxide solution is added to iron(III) chloride. *See:* gelatinous precipitate, granular precipitate.

preservative: a substance that prevents the natural organic decay processes from occurring. Many substances can be used safely for this purpose, including sulphites and nitrogen gas.

pressure: the force per unit area measured in pascals. *See:* pascal, atmospheric pressure.

product: a substance produced by a chemical reaction. *Example:* when the reactants copper and oxygen react, they produce the product, copper oxide.

proton: a positively charged particle in the nucleus of an atom that balances out the charge of the surrounding electrons.

proton number: this is the modern expression for atomic number. *See:* atomic number.

purify: to remove all impurities from a mixture, perhaps by precipitation, or filtration.

pyrolysis: chemical decomposition brought about by heat. *Example:* decomposition of lead nitrate. *See:* destructive distillation.

pyrometallurgy: refining a metal from its ore using heat. A blast furnace or smelter is the main equipment used.

quantitative: measurement of the amounts of constituents of a substance, for example by mass or volume. *See:* gravimetric analysis, volumetric analysis.

radiation: the exchange of energy with the surroundings through the transmission of waves or particles of energy. Radiation is a form of energy transfer that can happen through space; no intervening medium is required (as would be the case for conduction and convection).

radical: an atom, molecule, or ion with at least one unpaired electron. *Example:* nitrogen monoxide (NO).

radioactive: emitting radiation or particles from the nucleus of its atoms.

radioactive decay: a change in a radioactive element due to loss of mass through radiation. For example, uranium decays (changes) to lead.

reactant: a starting material that takes part in, and undergoes, change during a chemical reaction. *Example:* hydrochloric acid and calcium carbonate are reactants; the reaction produces the products calcium chloride, carbon dioxide and water.

reaction: the recombination of two substances using parts of each substance to produce new substances. *Example:* the reactants sodium chloride and sulphuric acid react and recombine to form the products sodium sulphate, chlorine and water.

reactivity: the tendency of a substance to react with other substances. The term is most widely used in comparing the reactivity of metals. Metals are arranged in a reactivity series.

reactivity series: the series of metals organised in order of their reactivity, with the most reactive metals, such as sodium, at the top and the least react metals, such as gold, at the bottom. Hydrogen is usually included in the series for comparative purposes.

reagent: a commonly available substance (reactant) used to create a reaction. Reagents are the chemicals normally kept on chemistry laboratory benches. Many substances called reagents are most commonly used for test purposes.

redox reaction (oxidation–reduction reaction): a reaction that involves oxidation and reduction; a reactions in which electrons are transferred. *See:* oxidation–reduction.

reducing agent: a substance that gives electrons to another substance being reduced (and therefore itself being oxidised) in a redox reaction. *Example:* hydrogen sulphide (H_2S).

reduction: the removal of oxygen from, or the addition of hydrogen to, a compound. Also a reaction in which an atom, ion or molecule gains electrons from an reducing agent. (The opposite of reduction is oxidation.)

reduction tube: a boiling tube with a small hole near the closed end. The tube is mounted horizontally, a sample is placed in the tube and a reducing gas, such as carbon monoxide, is passed through the tube. The oxidised gas escapes through the small hole.

refining: separating a mixture into the simpler substances of which it is made.

reflux distillation system: a form of distillation using a Liebig condenser placed vertically, so that all the vapours created during boiling are condensed back into the liquid, rather than escaping. In this way, the concentration of all the reactants remains constant.

relative atomic mass: in the past a measure of the mass of an atom on a scale relative to the mass of an atom of hydrogen, where hydrogen is 1. Nowadays a measure of the mass of an atom relative to the mass of one twelfth of an atom of carbon-12. If the relative atomic mass is given as a rounded figure, it is called an approximate relative atomic mass. *Examples*: chlorine 35, calcium 40, gold 197. *See:* atomic mass, atomic weight.

reversible reaction: a reaction in which the products can be transformed back into their original chemical form. *Example:* heated iron reacts with steam to produce iron oxide and hydrogen. If the hydrogen is passed over this heated oxide, it forms iron and steam. $3Fe + 4H_2O \rightleftharpoons Fe_3O_4 + 4H_2$.

roast: heating a substance for a long time at a high temperature, as in a furnace.

rust: the product of the corrosion of iron and steel in the presence of air and water.

salt: a compound, often involving a metal, that is the reaction product of an acid and a base, or of two elements. (Note 'salt' is also the common word for sodium chloride, common salt or table salt.) *Example:* sodium chloride (NaCl) and potassium sulphate (K_2SO_4) *See:* acid salt, basic salt, normal salt.

salt bridge: a permeable material soaked in a salt solution that allows ions to be transferred from one container to another. The salt solution remains unchanged during this transfer. *Example:* sodium sulphate used as a salt bridge in a galvanic cell.

saponification: a reaction between a fat and a base that produces a soap.

saturated: a state in which a liquid can hold no more of a substance. If any more of the substance is added, it will not dissolve.

saturated hydrocarbon: a hydrocarbon in which the carbon atoms are held with single bonds. *Example:* ethane (C_2H_6).

saturated solution: a solution that holds the maximum possible amount of dissolved material. When saturated, the rate of dissolving solid and that of recrystallisation solid are the same, and a condition of equilibrium is reached. The amount of material in solution varies with the temperature; cold solutions can hold less dissolved solid material than hot solutions. Gases are more soluble in cold liquids than in hot liquids.

sediment: material that settles out at the bottom of a liquid when it is still. A precipitate is one form of sediment.

semiconductor: a material of intermediate conductivity. Semiconductor devices often use silicon when they are made as part of diodes, transistors or integrated circuits. Elements intermediate between metals and non-metals are also sometimes called semiconductors. *Example:* germanium oxide, germanium. *See:* metalloid.

semipermeable membrane: a thin material that acts as a fine sieve or filter, allowing small molecules to pass, but holding large molecules back.

separating column: used in chromatography. A tall glass tube containing a porous disc near the base and filled with a substance (for example, aluminium oxide, which is known as a stationary phase) that can adsorb materials on its surface. When a mixture is passed through the column, fractions are retarded by differing amounts, so that each fraction is washed through the column in sequence.

separating funnel: a pear-shaped, glassware funnel designed to permit the separation of immiscible liquids by simply pouring off the more dense liquid while leaving the less dense liquid in the funnel.

series circuit: an electrical circuit in which all of the components are joined end to end in a line.

shell: the term used to describe the imaginary ball-shaped surface outside the nucleus of an atom that would be formed by a set of electrons of similar energy. The outermost shell is known as the valence shell. *Example:* neon has shells containing 2 and 8 electrons.

side-arm boiling tube: a boiling tube with an integral glass pipe near its open end. The side arm is normally used for the entry or exit of a gas.

simple distillation: the distillation of a substance when only one volatile fraction is to be collected. Simple distillation uses a Liebig condenser arranged almost horizontally. When the liquid mixture is heated and vapours are produced, they enter the condenser and then flow away from the flask and can be collected. *Example:* simple distillation of ethanoic acid.

slag: a mixture of substances that are waste products of a furnace. Most slags are composed mainly of silicates.

smelting: roasting a substance in order to extract the metal contained in it.

smog: a mixture of smoke and fog. The term is used to describe city fogs in which there is a large proportion of particulate matter (tiny pieces of carbon from exhausts) and also a high concentration of sulphur and nitrogen gases and probably ozone. *See:* photochemical smog.

smokeless fuel: a fuel which has been subjected to partial pyrolysis, such that there is no more loose particulate matter remaining. *Example:* Coke is a smokeless fuel.

solid/solid phase: a rigid form of matter which maintains its shape, whatever its container.

solubility: the maximum amount of a substance that can be contained in a solvent.

soluble: readily dissolvable in a solvent.

solute: a substance that has dissolved. *Example:* sodium chloride in water.

solution: a mixture of a liquid (the solvent) and at least one other substance of lesser abundance (the solute). Mixtures can be separated by physical means, for example, by evaporation and cooling. *See:* aqueous solution.

solvent: the main substance in a solution.

spectator ions: the ionic part of a compound that does not play an active part in a reaction. *Example:* when magnesium ribbon is placed in copper(II) sulphate solution, the copper is displaced from the solution by the magnesium, while the sulphate ion (SO_4^{2-}) plays no part in the reaction and so behaves as a spectator ion.

spectrum: a progressive series arranged using a characteristic etc. *Examples:* the range of colours that make up visible light (as seen in a rainbow) or across all electromagnetic radiation, arranged in progression according to their wavelength.

spontaneous combustion: the effect of a very reactive material or combination of reactants that suddenly reach their ignition temperature and begin to combust rapidly.

standard temperature and pressure (STP): 0°C at one atmosphere (a pressure which supports a column of mercury 760 mm high). Also given as 0°C at 100 kilopascals. *See:* atmospheric pressure.

state of matter: the physical form of matter. There are three states of matter: liquid, solid and gaseous.

stationary phase: a name given to a material which is used as a medium for separating a liquid mixture in chromatography.

strong acid: an acid that has completely dissociated (ionised) in water. Mineral acids are strong acids.

sublime/sublimation: the change of a substance from solid to gas, or vice versa, without going through a liquid phase. *Example:* iodine sublimes from a purple solid to a purple gas.

substance: a type of material, including mixtures.

sulphate: a compound that includes sulphur and oxygen and contains more oxygen than a sulphite. Sulphate ions have the chemical formula SO_4^{2-}. *Examples:* calcium sulphate $CaSO_4$ (the main

constituent of gypsum) and aluminium sulphate $Al_2(SO_4)_3$ (an alum).

sulphide: a sulphur compound that contains no oxygen. Sulphide ions have the chemical formula S^{2-}. *Example:* hydrogen sulphide (H_2S).

sulphite: a compound that includes sulphur and oxygen but contains less oxygen than a sulphate. Sulphite ions have the chemical formula SO_3^{2-}. *Example:* sodium sulphite Na_2SO_3.

supercooling: the ability of some substances to cool below their normal freezing point. *Example:* sodium thiosulphate.

supersaturated solution: a solution in which the amount of solute is greater than that which would normally be expected in a saturated solution. Most solids are more soluble in hot solutions than in cold. If a hot saturated solution is made up, the solution can be rapidly cooled down below its freezing point before it begins to solidify. This is a supersaturated solution.

surface tension: the force that operates on the surface of a liquid and which makes it act as though it were covered with an invisible, elastic film.

suspension: a mist of tiny particles in a liquid.

synthesis: a reaction in which a substance is formed from simpler reactants. *Example:* hydrogen gas and chlorine gas react to sythesise hydrogen chloride gas. The term can also be applied to polymerisation of organic compounds.

synthetic: does not occur naturally but has to be manufactured. Commonly used in the name 'synthetic fibre'.

tare: an allowance made for the weight of a container.

tarnish: a coating that develops as a result of the reaction between a metal and substances in the air. The most common form of tarnishing is a very thin, transparent oxide coating.

terminal: one of the electrodes of a battery.

test (chemical): a reagent or a procedure used to reveal the presence of another reagent. *Example:* litmus and other indicators are used to test the acidity or alkalinity of a substance.

test tube: A thin, glass tube, closed at one end and used for chemical tests, etc. The composition and thickness of the glass is such that, while it is inert to most chemical reactions, it may not sustain very high temperatures but can usually be heated in a Bunsen flame. *See:* boiling tube.

thermal decomposition: the breakdown of a substance using heat. *See* pyrolysis.

thermoplastic: a plastic that will soften and can be moulded repeatedly into shape on heating and will set into the moulded shape as it cools.

thermoset: a plastic that will set into a moulded shape as it cools, but which cannot be made soft by reheating.

thistle funnel: a narrow tube, expanded at the top into a thistlehead-shaped vessel. It is used as a funnel when introducing small amounts of liquid reactant. When fitted with a tap, it can be used to control the rate of entry of a reactant. *See:* burette.

titration: the analysis of the composition of a substance in a solution by measuring the volume of that solution (the titrant, normally in a burette) needed to react with a given volume of another solution (the titrate, normally placed in a flask). An indicator is often used to signal

change. *Example:* neutralisation of sodium hydroxide using hydrochloric acid in an acid–base titration. *See:* end point.

toxic: poisonous.

transition metals: the group of metals that belong to the d-block of the Periodic Table. Transition metals commonly have a number of differently coloured oxidation states. *Examples:* iron, vanadium.

Universal Indicator: a mixture of indicators commonly used in the laboratory because of its reliability. Used as a solution or impregnated into paper (Indicator paper), which is dampened before use. Universal Indicator changes colour from purple in a strongly alkaline solution through green when the solution is neutral to red in strongly acidic solutions. Universal Indicator is more accurate than litmus paper but less accurate than a pH meter.

unsaturated hydrocarbon: a hydrocarbon, in which at least one bond is a double or triple bond. Hydrogen atoms can be added to unsaturated compounds to form saturated compounds. *Example:* ethene, C_2H_4 or $CH_2=CH_2$.

vacuum: a container from which air has been removed using a pump.

valency: the number of bonds that an atom can form. *Examples:* calcium has a valency of 2 and bromine a valency of 1

valency shell: the outermost shell of an atom. *See:* shell.

vapour: the gaseous phase of a substance that is a liquid or a solid at that temperature. *Examples:* water vapour is the gaseous form of water, iodine vapour is the gaseous form of solid iodine. *See:* gas.

vein: a fissure in rock that has filled with ore or other mineral-bearing rock.

viscous: slow-moving, syrupy. A liquid that has a low viscosity is said to be mobile.

volatile: readily forms a gas.

volatile fraction: the part of a liquid mixture that will vaporise readily under the conditions prevailing during the reaction. *See:* fraction, vapour.

water of crystallisation: the water molecules absorbed into the crystalline structure as a liquid changes to a solid. *Example:* hydrated copper(II) sulphate $CuSO_4 \bullet 5H_2O$. *See:* hydrate.

weak acid and **weak base**: an acid or base that has only partly dissociated (ionised) in water. Most organic acids are weak acids. *See:* organic acid.

weight: the gravitational force on a substance. *See:* mass.

X-rays: a form of very short wave radiation.

MASTER INDEX